BRAZILIAN SKETCHES

REV. T. B. RAY, D.D.

Educational Secretary of the Foreign Mission Board of
the Southern Baptist Convention.

1st WORLD
LIBRARY
Literary Society

Brazilian Sketches

T. B. Ray

© 1st World Library, 2008
PO Box 2211
Fairfield, IA 52556
www.1stworldlibrary.com
First Edition

LCCN: 2007935413

Softcover ISBN: 978-1-4218-9363-1
Hardcover ISBN: 978-1-4218-9463-8
eBook ISBN: 978-1-4218-9263-4

Purchase *"Basil"*
as a traditional bound book at:
www.1stWorldLibrary.com/purchase.asp?ISBN=978-1-4218-9363-1

1st World Library is a literary, educational organization
dedicated to:

- Creating a free internet library of downloadable ebooks

- Hosting writing competitions and offering book publishing
  scholarships.

1ˢᵗ World Library Literary Society

Giving Back to the World

"If you want to work on the core problem, it's early school literacy."

- James Barksdale, former CEO of Netscape

"No skill is more crucial to the future of a child, or to a democratic and prosperous society, than literacy."

- Los Angeles Times

"Literacy... means far more than learning how to read and write... The aim is to transmit... knowledge and promote social participation."

- UNESCO

"Literacy is not a luxury, it is a right and a responsibility. If our world is to meet the challenges of the twenty-first century we must harness the energy and creativity of all our citizens."

- President Bill Clinton

"Parents should be encouraged to read to their children, and teachers should be equipped with all available techniques for teaching literacy, so the varying needs and capacities of individual kids can be taken into account."

- Hugh Mackay

TO MY WIFE WHO SHARED THE JOURNEY WITH ME

CONTENTS

FOREWORD 7

I. THE COUNTRY 10

II. THE CAPITAL, RIO DE JANEIRO....................13

III. A VISIT TO A COUNTRY CHURCH..............20

IV. TWO PRESIDENTS...25

V. THE GOSPEL WITHHELD 30

VI. SAINT WORSHIP..35

VII. PENANCE AND PRIEST 42

VIII. THE GOSPEL TRIUMPHANT 48

IX. JOSE BARRETTO 56

X. CAPTAIN EGYDIO 61

XI. FELICIDADE (Felicity) 71

XII. PERSECUTION 75

XIII. THE BIBLE AS A MISSIONARY FACTOR 82

XIV. THE METTLE OF THE NATIVE CHRISTIAN 88

XV. THE TESTING OF THE MISSIONARY 95

XVI. THE URGENT CALL 102

XVII. THE LAST STAND OF THE LATIN RACE............ 108

APPENDIX... 115

FOREWORD

I was dining one day with a very successful business man who, although his business had extensive relations in many lands, was meagerly informed about the work of missions. I thought I might interest him by telling him something of the effects of missions upon commerce. So I told him about how the civilizing presence of missionary effort creates new demands which in turn increases trade. He listened comprehendingly for a while and then remarked: "What you say is interesting, but what I wish to know is not whether missions increase business—we have business enough and have methods of increasing the volume—What I want to know is whether the missionary is making good and whether Christianity is making good in meeting the spiritual needs of the heathen. If ever I should become greatly interested in missions it would be because I should feel that Christianity could solve the spiritual problem for the heathen better than anything else. What are the facts about that phase of missions?"

These words made a profound impression on me, and since then I have spent little time in setting forth the by-products of missions, tremendously important and interesting though they are. I place the main emphasis on how gloriously Christianity, through the efforts of the missionary, meets the aching spiritual hunger of the heathen heart and transforms his life into spiritual efficiency.

Since this is my conception of what the burden of the message concerning missions should be, it should not surprise anyone to find the following pages filled with concrete statements of actual gospel triumphs. I have endeavored to draw a picture of the religious situation in Brazil by reciting facts. I have described some of the work of others done in former years and I have recorded some wonderful manifestations of the triumphant power of the gospel which I was privileged to see with my own eyes. These pages record testimony which thing, I take it, most people desire concerning the missionary enterprise. More arguments might have been stated and more conclusions might have been expressed, but I have left the reader to make his own deductions from the facts I have tried faithfully to record.

No attempt has been made to follow in detail the itinerary taken by my wife and myself which carried us into Brazil, Argentina and Chili in South America, and Portugal and Spain in Europe. It is sufficient to know that we reached the places mentioned and can vouch for the truth of the facts stated.

I have confined myself to sketches about Brazil because I did not desire to write a book of travel, but to show how the gospel succeeds in a Catholic field as being an example of the manner in which it is succeeding in other similar lands where it is being preached vigorously.

I wish to say also that I have drawn the materials from the experiences of my own denomination more largely because I know it better and therefore could bear more reliable testimony. It should be borne in mind that the successes of this one denomination are typical of the work of several other Protestant bodies now laboring in Brazil.

The missionaries and other friends made it possible wherever we went to observe conditions at close range and under favorable auspices. To these dear friends who received us so cordially and labored so untiringly for our comfort and to make our visit most helpful we would express here our heartfelt gratitude. We record their experiences and ours in the hope that the knowledge of them may bring to the reader a better appreciation of the missionary and the great cause for which the missionary labors so self-sacrificingly.

Richmond, Va.

CHAPTER I

THE COUNTRY

We had sailed in a southeasternly direction from New York twelve days when we rounded Cape St. Roque, the easternmost point of South America. A line drawn due north from this point would pass through the Atlantic midway between Europe and America. If we had sailed directly south we should have touched the western instead of the eastern coast, for the reason that practically the entire continent of South America lies east of the parallel of longitude which passes through New York.

After sighting land we sailed along the coast three days before we cast anchor at Bahia, our first landing place. Two days more were required to reach Rio de Janeiro. When we afterwards sailed from Rio to Buenos Aires, Argentina, we spent three and one-half days skirting along the shore of Brazil. For eight and one-half days we sailed in sight of Brazilian territory, and had we been close enough to shore north of Cape St. Roque, we should have added three days more to our survey of these far-stretching shores. Brazil lies broadside to the Atlantic Ocean with a coast line almost as long as the Pacific and Atlantic seaboards of the United States combined. Its ocean frontage is about 4,000 miles in length.

Rev. T. B. Ray

This coast line, however, is not all the water front of Brazil. She boasts of the Amazon, the mightiest river in the world. This stream is navigable by ships of large draught for 2,700 miles from its mouth. It has eight tributaries from 700 to 1,200 miles and four from 1,500 to 2,000 miles in length. One of these, the Madeira, empties as much water into the larger stream as does the Mississippi into the Gulf. No other river system drains vaster or richer territory. It drains one million square miles more than does the Mississippi, and in all it has 27,000 miles of navigable waters.

The land connections of Brazil are also extensive. All the other countries on the continent, save Chili and Ecuador, border on Brazil. The Guianas and Venezuela, on the north; Colombia and Peru on the west; Bolivia, Argentina, Paraguay and Uruguay on the south—eight countries in all.

It is indeed a vast territory. The United States could be placed within its borders and still there would be left enough Brazilian territory to make a State as large as Texas.

Almost from the time we sighted land until we rounded the cape near Montevideo, we could see the mountains along the shore. The mountains extend far interior and up and down the length of the country. The climate of the tropical Amazon Valley is, of course, very hot, but as soon as the mountains are reached on the way south the climate even in the tropical section is modified. The section south of Rio, on account of the mountains and other forces of nature, has a temperate climate, delightful for the habitation of man. Each of these great zones, the tropical, the subtropical and the temperate, is marked more by its distinctive leading products than by climate. Each of these sections yields a product in which Brazil leads the world. The largest and most inexhaustible rubber supply in the world is found in the Amazon Valley region. The central section raises so much cocoa that it gives

Brazil first rank in the production of this commodity. The great temperate region produces three-fourths of all the coffee used in the world. Of course, there is much overlapping in the distribution of these products. Other products, such as cotton, farinha, beans, peas, tobacco, sugar, bananas, are raised in large quantities and could be far more extensively produced if the people would utilize the best methods and implements of modern agriculture. The mountains are full of ores and the forests of the finest timber, and the great interior has riches unknown to man. It has the most extensive unexplored region on earth. What the future holds for this marvelously endowed country, when her resources are revealed and brought to market, no one would dare predict. Few countries in the world would venture a claim to such immense riches.

CHAPTER II

THE CAPITAL, RIO DE JANEIRO

The city of Rio is the center of life in Brazil. We entered the Bay of Rio after nightfall on the sixth of June. The miles and miles of lights in the city of Rio on the one side, and of Nietheroy on the other, gave us the impression that we were in some gigantic fair grounds. Missionaries Entzminger, Shepard, Maddox and Mrs. Entzminger came aboard to welcome us and bring us ashore. We were taken to the Rio Baptist College and Seminary, where we were entertained in good old Tennessee style by the Shepards. This school building was built in 1849 by Dom Pedro II. for a school which was known as the "Boarding School of Dom Pedro II." It accommodated two hundred students. The Emperor supported the school. In 1887 the school was moved to larger quarters. Dr. Shepard is renting the property for our college, but our school like Dom Pedro's has outgrown these quarters and we are compelled to rent additional buildings some distance away to accommodate the increasing number of students. There are about three hundred students in all departments.

As we studied the situation at close range, we had it driven in upon us that one of the greatest needs in Brazil is the one Dr. Shepard and his co-laborers are trying to meet in this school.

Three-fourths of the population of Brazil cannot read. We need, above all things now, educated leaders. What a call is there for trained native pastors and evangelists! Some of the Seminary students have been preaching as many as twenty-one times a month in addition to carrying their studies in the school. Dr. Shepard has been forced to stop them from some of this preaching because it was preventing successful work in the class room. The need is so great that it is very difficult to keep the students from such work.

I must not go too far afield from the subject of this chapter, but I must take the time to say that nothing breaks down prejudice against the gospel more effectively than do the schools conducted by the various mission boards. One day a Methodist colporter entered a town in the interior of the State of Minas Geraes and began to preach and offer his Bibles for sale in the public square. Soon a fanatical mob was howling around him and his life was in imminent peril. Just as the excitement was at the highest two young men belonging to one of the best families in the place pressed through the crowd and, ascertaining that the man was a minister of the gospel, took charge of him and drove off the mob. They led the colporter to their home, which was the best in the town, and showed him generous hospitality. They invited the people in to hear him preach, and thus through their kindness the man and his message received a favorable hearing. It should be remembered, too, that these young men belonged to a very devout Roman Catholic family.

What was the secret of their actions? They had rescued, entertained and enabled to preach a man who was endeavoring to propagate a faith that was very much opposed to their own. The explanation is that they had attended Granberry College, that great Methodist school at Juiz de Fora. They had not accepted Protestant Christianity, but the school had given them such a vision and appreciation of the gospel that they could never again be the intolerant bigots their fellow townsmen were. The college had made them friends and that was a tremendous service. First we must have friends, then followers. Nothing more surely and more extensively makes friends for our cause than the schools, and it must be said also that they are wonderfully effective in the work of direct evangelization.

The First Baptist Church commissioned Deacon Theodore Teixeira and Dr. Shepard to pilot us over the city. The church provided us with an automobile and our splendid guides magnified their office. It is a MAGNIFICENT city, indeed. The strip of land between the mountains and the seashore is not wide. In some places, in fact, the mountains come quite down to the water. The city, in the most beautiful and picturesque way, avails itself of all possible space, even in many places climbing high on the mountain sides and pressing itself deep into the coves. Perhaps no city in the world has a more picturesque combination of mountain and water with which to make a beautiful location. It has about a million inhabitants, and being the federal capital, is the greatest and most influential city in Brazil.

Most of its streets are narrow and tortuous and until recently were considered unhealthy. A few years ago the magnificent Avenida Central was cut through the heart of the city and one of the most beautiful avenues in the world was built. Twelve million dollars' worth of property was condemned to make way for this splendid street. It cuts across a peninsula through the heart of the city from shore to shore, and is magnificent, indeed, with its sidewalks wrought in beautiful geometrical designs, with its ornate street lamps, with its generous width appearing broader by contrast with other narrow streets, with its modern buildings.

There is another street, however, which is dearer to the

Brazilian than the Avenida. He takes great pride in the Avenida, but he has peculiar affection for the Rua d'Ouvidor. Down the Ouvidor flows a human tide such as is found nowhere else in Brazil. No one attempts to keep on the pavement. The street is given over entirely to pedestrians. No vehicle ever passes down it until after midnight. In this narrow street, with its attractive shops filled with the highest-priced goods in the world, you can soon find anyone you wish to meet, because before long everyone who can reach it will pass through. In this street the happy, jesting, jostling crowd is in one continuous "festa".

In passing through the city one is greatly impressed by the number of parks and beautiful public squares, and in particular with the wonderful Beiramar, which is a combination of promenades, driveways and park effects that stretches for miles along the shore of the bay. What a thing of beauty this last-named park is! There is nothing comparable to it anywhere. When Rio wishes to go on a grand "passeio" (promenade) nothing but the grand Beiramar will suffice.

One cannot help being impressed also by the prevalence of coffee- drinking stands and stores—especially if he meets many friends. These friends will insist upon taking him into a coffee stand and engaging him in conversation while they sip coffee. On many corners are little round or octagonal pagoda-like structures in which coffee and cakes are sold. The coffee-drinking places are everywhere and most of them are usually filled. The practice of taking coffee with one's friends must lessen materially the amount of strong drink consumed by the Brazilian. Nevertheless, that amount of strong drink is, alas, altogether too great.

The greatest nuisance on the streets of Rio, or any other city of Brazil, is the lottery ticket seller. These venders are more numerous and more insistent than are the newsboys in the

United States. There are all sorts of superstitions about lotteries. Certain images in one's dreams at night are said to correspond to certain lucky numbers. Dogs, cats, horses, cows and many other animals have certain numbers corresponding to them. For instance, if one should dream tonight about a dog, he would try tomorrow to find a lottery ticket to correspond in number with a dog. Say the dog number was thirty-seven. This man would try to find a ticket whose number ends in thirty-seven. Such a ticket would be considered lucky. The ticket sellers often call out as they pass along the street the last two numbers on the tickets they have to sell, and if a man hears the number called which corresponds to the animal he dreamed about last night, he will consider it lucky and buy. There are also many shops where only lottery tickets are sold. No evil has more tenaciously and universally fastened upon the people than has the evil of gambling in lotteries. There are 310 Federal lotteries, besides many others run by the various States. These 310 lotteries receive in premiums the enormous sum of $19,399,200 every month—about one dollar for every individual in Brazil. A portion of the profits amassed by the lottery companies is devoted to charity, a portion to Roman Catholic churches and a portion goes to the government. Even after these amounts are taken out, there is ample left for the enrichment of the companies' coffers to the impoverishment of many very needy working people.

It is difficult to write temperately of Rio de Janeiro. There is such a rare combination here of the primitive and the progressive, of the oriental and occidental, that one is inclined to go off into exclamation points. On the Avenida Central one sees numbers of street venders carrying all kinds of wares on their heads and pulling all sorts of carts, making their way in and out among the automobiles, and handsome victorias PULLED BY MULES. We note also all types of people. The Latin features predominate, but the negro is in evidence, the Indian features are often recognized, and mingled with these are seen faces representing all nations. One is impressed with the dress of the people. Who is that handsomely- groomed, gentleman passing? From his fine clothes you think he must be a man of wealth and influence. Who is he? He is a barber. That one over there is a clerk. But why these fine clothes? Ah! thereby hangs the tale. Appearance is worshiped. Parade runs through everything, even in the prevailing religion, which, alas, is little more than form—parade. Don't get the idea that everybody is finely dressed and that every handsomely-dressed man is a barber. Many are able to afford such clothes and are cultured gentlemen. One notices most the dress of the lower classes, the most striking article of which is the wooden-bottom sandals into which they thrust their toes and go flapping along in imminent peril of losing the slippers every moment. The remainder of the clothing worn by these beslippered people consists often of only two thin garments. Certainly this is a place of great contrasts. But somehow these contrasts do not impress one as being incongruous. They are in perfect keeping with their surroundings. Rio is really a cosmopolitan city and is a pleasant blending of the old and the new.

There are several places from which splendid views of the city can be had, but none of them is comparable to the panorama which stretches out before one when he stands on the top of Mt. Corcovado. The scene which greets one from this mountain is indescribable. The Bay of Rio de Janeiro, with its eighty islands, Sugar Loaf Mountain, a bare rock standing at the entrance, the city winding its tortuous way in and out between the mountains and spreading itself over many hills, the open sea in the distance and the wild mountain scenery to the back of us, constitute a panorama surpassingly beautiful.

Nictheroy lies just across the bay. We went over there one night and spoke in the rented hall where our church worships, and spent the night in the delightful home of the Entzmingers. The next morning, before breakfast, Dr. Entzminger showed me over the city. Nictheroy has forty thousand inhabitants and is the capital of the State of Rio de Janeiro. It is a beautiful city and offers a wide field for missionary work. Its importance is apparent.

We have a church in the populous suburb of Engenho de Dentro. We were present there at a great celebration when the church cleared off the remainder of its debt and burned the notes. The building was crowded to its utmost capacity. The people stood in the aisles from the rear to the pulpit. They filled the little rooms behind the pulpit and occupied space about the windows. There are about seventy members of the church. A far greater progress should be made now that the debt as well as other encumbrances have been removed.

There are in Rio the First, Engenho de Dentro, Governors Island and Santa Cruz churches, and twelve preaching places, four of which are in rented halls. Missionary Maddox utilizes many members of the churches in providing preaching at these missions. There are only a very few paid evangelists in this mission, but a great many church members are glad to go to these stations and tell the gospel story.

Besides our Baptist work, the Southern Methodists are conducting a very prosperous mission. They have several churches and a station for settlement work. The Presbyterians and the Congregationalists have some excellent churches and the YMCA is one of the most flourishing in South America.

CHAPTER III

A VISIT TO A COUNTRY CHURCH

That I may give you a glimpse of the country life in Brazil, and also some impression of country mission work, I invite you to take a trip with Missionary Maddox and myself to the little hamlet of Parahyba do Sul, in the interior of the State of Rio.

On Monday, June 13th, we boarded a six AM train for Parahyba do Sul, which we reached about ten o'clock. It is a charming town situated on the river by the same name. This river reminds one of the French Broad, though the mountains are not so high and precipitous as the North Carolina mountains. The mountains, too, in this section are not covered with trees, but with a tall grass, which, being in bloom, gave a beautiful purple color to the landscape. The railroad climbs up the mountain sides from Rio in a very picturesque manner.

The Parahyba do Sul Church is three miles over the mountains from the station, in the house of Mrs. Manoela Rosa Rodrigues. The house is constructed with mud walls and a thatched roof. The floors are the bare ground, which is packed hard and smooth. There are two rooms, with a narrow hall between them and a sort of "lean to" kitchen.

The largest room, which is about fifteen feet square, is devoted to the church. The most prominent piece of furniture in the house is the pulpit, which stands in this room. This pulpit is large out of all proportion to everything else about the place. It was covered over with a beautifully embroidered altar piece. The two chairs placed for Brother Maddox and myself were also entirely covered with crocheted Brazilian lace. I hesitated to occupy such a daintily decorated seat.

This church of forty-six members maintains three Sunday schools in the adjoining country and six preaching stations, members of the church doing the preaching. Every member gives to the college in Rio 200 reis (six cents) a month, and to missions, etc., 300 reis (nine cents) per month. This is munificent liberality when we take into consideration their exhausting poverty.

Our coming was a great event with them. We were met at the station by a member of the church, who mounted us on a gray pony apiece and soon had us on our way. He walked, and with his pacing sort of stride he easily kept up with us. His feet were innocent of shoes. He says he does not like shoes because they interfere with his walking. Underneath that dilapidated hat and those somewhat seedy clothes we found a warm-hearted Christian, who serves the Lord with passionate devotion. He often preaches, though he has very little learning. He is mighty in the Scriptures, having committed to memory large sections of them, and has a genuine experience of grace to which he bears testimony with great power.

We arrived at the church about eleven o'clock. We were received with expressions of great joy. Mrs. Manoela was so happy over our coming that she embraced us in true Brazilian style. We were shown into our room, where we refreshed ourselves by brushing off the dust and bathing.

How spick and span clean was everything in that room, even to the dirt floor!

Before we had completed our ablutions, the good woman of the house called Maddox out and asked what she could cook for me. She thought I could not eat Brazilian dishes. He told her, to her great relief, that I could eat anything he could. Quite right he was, too, for we had been traveling all the morning on the sustenance furnished by a cup of coffee which we had taken at the Rio station a little before six o'clock. We were in possession of an appetite by this time that would have raised very few questions about any article of food.

Soon we were seated at the breakfast table, which was placed in the church room with benches around it for seats. I was honored by being placed at one end of the table. What a meal it was! Not only had Mrs. Manoela taxed her own larder, but the other members, who by this time had arrived in large numbers, had brought in many good things. I cannot tell what the dishes were, for the reason that I do not know. It is sufficient to say that every one was good—perhaps our appetite helped out our appreciation of some of them. There were as many as eight dishes the like of which I had never tasted before. How do you suppose I managed it when they served some delicious cane molasses, and, instead of bread to go with it, they served cream cheese? I asked Maddox how I should work this combination. He replied by cutting up his cheese into his plate of molasses and eating the mixture. I did the same thing, and I bear testimony that it was fine. By the time the breakfast was concluded, I had scored a point with our good friends, for they thought that a stranger who could render such a good account of himself at a Brazilian breakfast must be very much like themselves. (Let us explain about Brazilian meals: They take coffee in the early morning. Bread and butter is served with the coffee.

Breakfast, which is a very substantial meal, is served about eleven o'clock. Dinner, which is the chief meal of the day, is served about five o'clock in the afternoon. At bedtime light refreshments are served, which are often substantial enough to make another meal).

After breakfast was over, and it was some time before it was over, for the crowd had to be fed, we assembled for worship. The congregation was too large for the little room, so the men built a beautiful arbor out of bamboo cane. When Maddox told me we were to hold services under an arbor I was dissappointed, for somehow there had come over me a great desire to speak from that large pulpit in the little room. My dissappointment was short-lived, however, for when we reached the arbor there were the pulpit and the lace-covered chairs! It was a gracious service. The Spirit of the Lord was upon us. The sermon lost none of its effect from the fact that it had to be interpreted, because Maddox interpreted it with sympathy and power.

After preaching, four were received for baptism. They were not converted at this service, but had been expecting to come for some time. Maddox baptized them in the spring branch, which had been deepened by a temporary dam being thrown across it. One of those baptized was a woman ninety years of age.

Our time was growing short now. Maddox changed his clothes in a hurry. We had to catch the four o'clock train. We did stop long enough to drink a cup of Brazilian coffee. Such coffee! I will not attempt to describe it, because our friends in the States can not understand. There is nothing like it in this country. We took time, too, to say good-bye. The whole crowd lined up and we went the length of the line, bidding everyone a hearty godspeed. The Brazilian not only shakes hands with you, but he embraces you heartily. Yes, some of the good matrons embraced us. It was a novel experience for me, but a mere custom with them, and the act was performed with such modest restraint that any possible objectionable features were eliminated. Having said good-bye to them all we mounted our gray ponies, and, led by our barefooted friend, rode away with thanks-giving in our hearts for the good fellowship with the saints of Parahyba do Sul.

The tie of love for a common Lord had bound our affections to them. Their simple-hearted sincerity and devotion had helped us. Their zeal had contributed to our faith. One incident touched me especially. Just before breakfast a little girl about four years of age, led by her mother, brought to us a package containing some Brazilian cakes. When we opened the package there lay on top a piece of folded paper on Which was written: "How beautiful upon the mountains are the feet of him that bringeth good tidings, that publisheth peace, that bringeth good tidings of good, that publisheth salvation, that saith unto Zion, thy God reigneth' '(Isa. 52:7). Presented to our brother pastors, Maddox and Ray by Archimina Nunes." Instantly there arose in my heart the prayer that God would speed the day when his swift-footed messengers shall publish the good tidings of peace to all this vast and needy land.

CHAPTER IV

TWO PRESIDENTS

It was our good fortune while in Rio to be received by the President of the Republic, Dr. Nilo Pecanha. Missionaries Shepard, Langston and Ginsburg and Dr. Nogueira Paranagua escorted me. When we started I suggested that we take a street car. Not so those Brazilians! We must go in an automobile. We were very careful to wear our Prince Albert coats, too; for, above all things, the Brazilian is a master in punctilious ceremonies. We were ushered into the waiting room by a doorkeeper, a finely-liveried mulatto with a large chain around his shoulders to indicate his authority. The waiting room was full of people, but we were not kept waiting long. We sent in our cards and soon we heard our names announced and we were led into the presence of the private secretary. After a few words of explanation by Dr. Paranagua, the secretary retired to ask the President if he would see us. He returned presently and showed us into the audience chamber, which was a large and tastefully decorated room. Around the walls were several groups of chairs, placed in true Brazilian style somewhat as follows: A cane-bottomed divan was set with its back to the wall, then several cane-bottomed chairs were placed at right angles to it in two rows facing each other, usually four in a row. The President guided me between these chairs and took a seat on the divan and motioned me to a seat by his side. He is a man of slight build, with a mild expression which wins confidence. He was most informal in his speech and spoke in a candid and unreserved manner which quickly put us at ease.

I told him, through an interpreter, that we had come from a visit to the Minister of the Interior, with whom we had been in conference about the status of Brazilian schools. The President expressed his great pleasure over our coming to see him and said that he had personal knowledge of what our denomination is doing and of some of the workers. He was satisfied that our object was altruistic and for the good of the country and people; that so far as depended upon him, he was ready to give us the full benefit of his official position. As proof of his wish to see absolute religious freedom, he cited an instance of how he had protected some monks in the Amazon Valley recently. These men were in straits and he had sent soldiers to liberate them, and then turning with a smile to Ginsburg, he said that he also never abandoned his friend Solomon when he was attacked. He refreshed our minds upon the fact that lately, when certain priests in the city of Rio had attempted to resist the government over a disputed piece of property which had been granted them under the old regime, he gave them to understand that if they did not behave themselves, the door was open and they could leave the country. They soon came to terms. As to his successor, the President said that the incoming President was of the same party and would carry out the same policies, ideas and ideals. These policies meant absolute liberty of thought, conscience and speech, which is guaranteed by the constitution. Before the interview closed, he again expressed his pleasure at receiving a representative of an American institution, convinced as he was that the propaganda of our schools, morals and ideals would draw the two nations closer together, and that he was ready to encourage us to that end. "We are following the ideals of the United States", he said, "which we recognize as our elder sister." He expressed peculiar pleasure over the prospect of our establishing a college and he assured us that the Brazilian government would put no obstacle in the way of our purpose, but that it would do all in its power, on the other hand, to encourage us.

While we are meeting Presidents, I would like to introduce you to another one upon whom the salvation of Brazil depends more largely than it does upon any occupant of the chair of chief magistrate. It is possible for the man who has been elevated by the ballots of his people to serve in a large way the moral good of his people and we thank God for all rulers who rule with justice and liberality in the interest of liberty and the common good. But far greater and far more serviceable than these are those choice spirits who, by embracing the gospel of Christ, give themselves devoutly to bringing in His reign in the hearts of men. Such spirits, by the sheer force of their characters, wield a far more abiding influence for the help of their fellows. The man I wish to introduce is Dr. Nogueira Paranagua, the President of the Brazilian Baptist Convention.

He belongs to one of the oldest and most aristocratic families of the State of Piauhy. He was Governor of his state at the time of the institution of the Republic. After the establishment of the Republic, he was elected to the National Congress for a term of four years. Then he was elected to the Senate and served nine years. He is a skilled physician and is married to a Swiss lady of fine family. His family connections occupy one quarter of the State of Piauhy. He is, at the present time, Treasurer of the National Printing Concern, which does not occupy all of his time. The remainder of his time he devotes to the practice of his profession and to the preaching of the gospel. He is a deacon in the First church in Rio. He is not an ordained minister—he is simply an humble man of God. He is an ardent patriot who believes that the salvation of Brazil can be realized only through the gospel of Christ, to which he gives his life and all.

Now I, for one, believe that the theory of Dr. Nogueira is the one that will finally lead Brazil into the fullness of life and power it is capable of attaining. It is well to have written in the constitution the guarantee of religious and political liberty. It is well to have Presidents who courageously carry into effect the provisions of this constitution, but the highest good is not attained until behind all documentary guarantees is a personal righteousness in the people. Dr. Nogueira's insistent advocacy of Christ for Brazil is the one thing that gives assurance of a genuine righteousness that will exalt the nation.

He is the President of a remarkable body. It was our privilege to attend the Brazilian Baptist Convention which met in Sao Paulo, June, 1910. It was composed of sixty delegates, about one third of whom were missionaries. The remainder were natives. They came from all parts of Brazil. One man from the Madeira Valley traveled three weeks on his journey to Sao Paulo. They represented 109 churches, which had a total membership of 7,000. These churches increased by baptism twenty-five per cent, last year. They maintain a boys' school and a theological school at Pernambuco, a school for boys and girls at Bahia, a boys' school at Nova Friburgo, a girls' school at Sao Paulo and the crown of the school system, the Rio Baptist College and Seminary in the capital. They have a Publication Board to produce Sunday School and other literature, a Home Mission Board to develop the missionary work in the bounds of Brazil, and a Foreign Mission Board, which conducts foreign mission operations in Chill and Portugal. While their country is so needy, they believe in the principle of foreign missions so thoroughly that they gave last year for foreign missions as much per capita as did the churches in the bounds of the

Southern Baptist Convention. One night during the Convention, I addressed them upon the subject of foreign missions, and after I had finished speaking one of the missionaries came forward and said he had thought that in as much as he had given his life to foreign mission work, he was not under any special obligation to contribute money to this cause, but now he saw his error and proposed to give as a means of grace and in order to discharge his duty to the larger cause.

What a privilege it was to attend this Convention! All of us took our meals at the Girls' College and by this arrangement we had a most delightful time socially. It is a fine body full of good cheer, hope, faith, courage, consecration. To come to know them—missionaries and native Christians alike—is to enter into fellowship with some of the choicest and most indomitable spirits that have ever adorned the Kingdom of our Lord.

CHAPTER V

THE GOSPEL WITHHELD

When I went to South America I decided that I would spend little time upon the material aspects of the trip, but would, on the other hand, attempt to arrive at an understanding of the religious conditions and needs of the people. I consider that the religious needs are the abiding and vital interests of any people.

I knew also that Brazil is counted as being a Roman Catholic country and the consideration at once arose in connection with this fact as to whether this religion affected the life and thought of the people sufficiently to satisfy their religious needs. If it does, then let us be honest enough to recognize it, and if it does not, let us be courageous enough to assume our responsibility towards it for we must hold that the great justification for missionary effort is the evangelical and not the polemical one. If there is no greater reason for our entering a country than for the purpose of fighting the Catholics, then I, for one, am frank to say that I do not think we ought to spend our energies in any such field. The question for us to settle is whether there is a real call for the preaching of the gospel in a given country. That question can be answered only by a candid consideration of the facts in the case and not by the bigoted notion that all who do not

Rev. T. B. Ray

agree with us are to be driven from the face of the earth.

What is the religious status of Brazil? Is there any call for Protestant effort? I answer after giving serious study to this question, and after personal observation of the effects of the religious practices upon the people, that there is the same imperative call for missionary effort in Brazil that comes from China or any other heathen country, viz., the gospel is not preached to the people.

The priests hold services, to be sure, in the churches, but there are many churches in Brazil in which there has been no pretense of preaching a sermon within five years. The priests do not preach. They say mass, read prayers and sing songs in Latin, a language which is not understood by the people. Occasionally, a Catholic fraternity will invite a special orator to preach a sermon upon some great feast day. This visiting brother does not preach. His theme upon such an occasion would either be a discussion of the special saint whose day is being celebrated, or he would speak upon some civic question which had more or less to do with the moral or political life of the people. In the interior these special occasions occur only once every two to five years, so that even this semblance of a sermon comes rarely. In the cities these special addresses are made on one saint's day each year or on some special anniversary, or when some dignitary is making a visit. Usually this dignitary will say a mass and not preach. When one of these special days occurs the preaching is not heard very extensively for the reason that the noise and commotion about the stalls for gambling, drinking and other attractions is sufficient to drown the voice of the speaker. These side-show attractions fill all available space about the building, giving it the appearance of a circus more than anything else. They are run by individuals who pay a tax to the church for the privilege. The preaching is not the feature of the day, the chief object seeming to be to furnish amusement for the people and money for the church. It cannot be said that on such days the gospel can possibly be preached successfully.

Occasionally there is held in the church what is called a special mission. This is conducted by visiting monks. We would expect that on such occasions the gospel would be preached, but such is not the case. They hear confessions in the morning. A special premium is placed upon the celebration of marriages during the mission, because these visiting monks will make a cheaper rate than the resident priests. For this reason the majority of the priests do not like to have these monks come in for special missions, and would not conduct them but for the fact that the bishop compels them to do so. The addresses delivered by the monks in these special missions are not sermons. They either upbraid the Protestants, speak against civil marriage (the only legal marriage in Brazil is that performed by a civil officer), inveigh against the Republic, discourse upon the lives of the saints, assail Luther and other reformers, or urge confession, penance and submission to the Pope.

Furthermore, the Bible is withheld from the people. The circulation of no book is so bitterly opposed as that of the Bible. It is true that the Franciscan monks are trying to introduce an edition of the New Testament which contains special comments attacking Protestants. These special editions are very expensive and difficult to secure. The person who wishes to buy one of these Bibles must get permission from the vicar of his parish, and if the would-be purchaser is inclined towards Protestantism, the vicar will refuse to grant permission. The priests are not very much in sympathy with the idea of circulating even this annotated edition of the New Testament.

In Armagoza, near Bahia, the Franciscan monks held, three

or four years ago, a mission and sold about 1,000 of these Catholic Scriptures. It seems that the Protestants had also been circulating a Testament which had the same general appearance as that sold by the Franciscan monks. When the monks had sold out their supplies, they heard of what the Protestants had done and inasmuch as the people could not distinguish between the true book and the false, they ordered the people to bring back all of the books to the monks, under the promise that they would examine them, eliminate the Protestant book and return to the owners the authorized Bible. The people brought back their books in good faith. The monks took them, but never returned them. Neither did they return the money.

On the 22nd of February, 1903, there occurred a public burning of Bibles in Pernambuco. This was done in defiance of the Protestant work with the evident purpose of intimidating the Protestant workers and arousing a public sentiment against them.

But having failed in this, their first effort, they decided to try another even more ostentatious.

Although it is illegal to burn any religious document publicly, yet the first burning passed unnoticed by the officials of the law. But not so the second.

Having incurred the censure and ill-will of many of the most thoughtful and liberal-minded, even of the Catholics themselves, by the disgrace of February 22nd, the directors of the Anti- Protestant League decided to make a grand rally on the occasion of the league's first anniversary, September 27th. And to realize this, they published about two weeks beforehand a very extensive program. The program said that "there will be burned 26 Bibles, 42 Testaments, 45 copies of the Gospel of Matthew, Luke 9, John 12, Mark 4 and Acts

9", besides a great many other useful books. In the list also there were some three hundred copies of different religious Protestant papers.

According to the program the bishop was to preside. The public burning, however, was not performed. Such pressure was brought to bear upon the officials that they interfered. It was even discussed in the National House of Congress. But in spite of all opposition, not to be completely defeated, they burned the Bibles in the back yard of the church.

These examples are sufficient to demonstrate the attitude of the priests towards the Scriptures, and we must concede that any church or set of men who by such methods withhold from the people the Word of God cannot be said to preach the gospel. He is an enemy of the gospel who puts any restraint upon the circulation of the Scriptures. It is wise indeed for the sake of their cause that these opponents of Protestantism should oppose the circulation of the Scriptures, for we shall cite numerous instances of how the Bible unaided has broken down Romish superstition and turned men from dark error into the light of the glorious gospel of Jesus.

Rev. T. B. Ray

CHAPTER VI

SAINT WORSHIP

What is the real religion of the Brazilians? It is more a saint worship than anything else. Saint worship is at its core. Mary is the chief saint. All prayers are made to her. She is the intercessor. The Litany is all addressed to Mary. It runs, "Oh Mary, hear us, etc." She is worshiped under different aspects —Mary of the Sailors, Mary of the Conception, Mary of the Candles, Mary of the Rosary, ad infinitum. Even Christ is worshiped as a saint. The patron saint of Campos, for instance, is called Sao Salvador (St. Savior). The city of Bahia is called Sao Salvador. Its patron saint is Jesus.

A saint is an intercessor between man and God. Because of his holiness, he has favor with God, and therefore the people pray to him. Very few consider the saint lower than God. They offer sacrifices, make prayers and burn candles to the saint.

St. Anthony of Padua is a very hard-worked saint. He has placed upon him the double duty of furnishing suitors for all the young women and of leading the armies of the Republic to victory. No wonder this overworked saint gets into trouble. Young women place him in their rooms, burn candles and offer prayers before him. He is dressed up in the finest toggery and is given great honor. If, however, after awhile he does not bring along the suitor, he is given a sound beating, or he may be hung head downwards in a well or stood on his head under a table. These indignities are heaped upon him in order to force him to produce the suitor which the young lady very much desires. He is also the military saint. In the time of the Empire, he was carried at the head of the army and had the rank of a colonel. Even after the Empire was abolished, he retained his rank for many years and received from the government the salary of a colonel. Such an idol was in Bahia and his salary was discontinued only five years ago. The money went, of course, to the priest in the church where the image was kept.

Every town, village and country seat has its protecting saint. In time of drouth they in many places carry the saint through the streets in procession. He is taken from his place in the church to some hut, maybe, where he is placed beneath the altar. This is done in order to cause him to bring rain. After the rain comes he is taken out and with great distinction is replaced in his original niche. They do this sometimes in the case of a scourge of insects or disease.

Late one evening, after Missionary Ginsburg and I had returned from a trip into the interior of the State of Bahia, we arrived in the city of Nazareth. It is a town of about 10,000 inhabitants. We were to wait here until the following morning for the boat which was to take us to Bahia.

As we went down the street we saw a great throng of people surging about an image which was being carried upon the shoulders of some men. Two priests walked in front to direct the movements of the procession. More than half of the people in the city must have been in the procession. They paraded far out into the country, crossed to the opposite side of the river, wound themselves back and forth through the narrow streets until a late hour at night. At eleven o'clock just before we retired, we stood for some time watching the procession pass the hotel where we were stopping. It was a miserably ugly little image, gaudily decorated. It was being paraded through the streets for the purpose of staying the plague of smallpox, which at that time was scourging the town. When we saw the procession last it had been augmented by such numbers that it appeared as if the entire city was following this image. They seemed to believe that it could really charm away the smallpox.

This is not an isolated case. It is typical. Every patron saint has laid upon him at times the responsibility of breaking a drouth or the effects of a dreadful scourge which may be afflicting the people. It is the veriest sort of idolatry.

One of the most pitiful exhibitions of superstition to be found in Brazil is that in connection with the many shrines to which pilgrimages are made by thousands of people and at which places great miracles are supposed to be performed. In Bahia there is a famous shrine called Bom Fim (Good End). It is located on a hill in the suburbs of the city. Years ago tradition has it, the image of San Salvador was found on the summit of this hill. A priest took charge of the image and removed it to a church. On the following morning the image was missing, and upon going to the spot where he first found it, he discovered the image. Again he took it to the church, and again on the following day, he found the image at the original place. The tradition was, therefore, started that the image had fallen from Heaven to the top of the hill, and every time it was removed from this spot it, of itself, returned. So it was taken for granted that the image desired its shrine built on this spot. At first there was a little shrine constructed, and afterward was built the magnificent edifice which now shelters the image.

To this place the thousands go annually upon pilgrimages. One of the most gruesome spectacles to be found anywhere is in a side room near the altar. From the ceiling are suspended wax and plaster of paris reproductions called ex-votos of literally every portion of the body—feet, hands, limbs, heads, all portions—the ceiling space is completely covered with these uncanny figures. The wall is hung with pictures, which portray all sorts of scenes, such as a man in shipwreck, a carpenter falling down a ladder, a child falling out of a second-story window, death chambers of various people, etc. These figures and pictures are intended to represent miracles. When these people were in their afflictions they prayed to the image of the Good End and made a promise that if they should recover they would bring one of these votive offerings of the part affected, whether of man or beast, to the shrine. Some of them came before the cure was effected, and with a prayer, left the image behind and the cures of their disease or afflictions were attributed to the image of Bom Fim. It is said that when this church is given its annual cleaning, just before the celebration of the saint's day, thousands of people congregate here, roll in the waters which are used to wash out the building, and drink the filthy stuff, deeming it to be holy. There is hardly a more revolting scene to be found anywhere, and all in the name of religion. Until recently, when the police put an end to it, a most disgusting species of holy dance was observed on this annual day in which the most sensual practices were indulged.

Perhaps the most famous shrine in all Brazil is in the far interior of the State of Bahia on the San Francisco River. It is the famous Lapa. The image has its shrine in a cave in a very remarkable geological formation. One hundred thousand people make pilgrimages to this shrine every year from all of the States in Brazil. The last Emperor himself made a visit to this shrine. From June to August of last year $20,000 was collected from the pilgrims. Our missionary, Jackson, met a man who had been on the way six months. It required him a year to make this trip. The same missionary saw a family from the State of Alagoas which had been on the journey six weeks. Dr. Z. C. Taylor says he passed through sections that had been almost depopulated because the men had sold out their homes, horses and cattle in order to seek a miracle in their favor at this same shrine. Fire destroyed the image in 1902. Protestants were accused of setting fire to it because a missionary was near at the time. (He was forty miles away.) In the controversy that arose the missionary noted that, inasmuch as the new image was sent by freight and not by ticket, it must be an idol and not a saint. Suffice it to say, that a new image was placed and the people are worshiping it with the same zeal with which they worshiped the old, even though the new one came by freight and the old one was supposed to have fallen from Heaven. It is believed to have miracle working power and to give great merit to one who makes the pilgrimage to it.

In the daily paper called the "Provinca," published in Pernambuco, there was printed on August 23, 1910, the following telegram from the city of Rio, the capital of the Republic.

"The Seculo (Century) of today announces that on St. Leopold street in Andarahy (a suburb of Rio) there was discovered a fountain of water in a hollow rock, in which a plebian found an image of a saint.

"This image," adds the Seculo, "although in water, did not present the least vestige of humidity. The news of this curious discovery was immediately circulated, and there was a great pilgrimage, including a reporter of the Seculo, to this miraculous fountain in Andarahy."

It is very probable that this telegram heralds the advent of a new shrine, because it is in this fashion that these so-called miracle-working shrines are brought into existence.

Not all of these shrines are canonized, but nevertheless they have power over the people. As we were making a trip into the interior of the State of Pernambuco we passed a station called Severino. Near the station we could see a splendid church building which had been constructed in honor of St. Severino. This saint is not in the calendar, not recognized by the church nor the bishop, yet it is popular all over Brazil. Many people are named after him, and to this shrine are brought many of the same sort of things as were described in connection with the shrine of the Good End. This idol is stuffed with sugar-cane pith. The head of it was found in the woods some time ago. A tradition was started that an image had fallen from Heaven. The superstitious people believed the report and soon a shrine was in full operation, which today, even though it be not canonized, is exerting a far-reaching influence. The owner of the shrine gave up his farming and lives handsomely on the offerings the deluded bring to his private shrine.

In one of the most magnificent churches in Bahia is an image of a negro saint. This holy being won his canonization as a reward for stealing money from his master to contribute to the church. That is it: Do anything you please, provided you share the spoils with the church.

Across the breast of the Virgin's image in the church of Our Lady of Penha in Pernambuco, before which church the Bibles were burned in 1903, are written the following words: "One hundred days' indulgence to the person who will kiss the holy foot of the Holy Virgin." This pitifully expresses, perhaps, the thought behind saint worship. It is the hope that the aching of the sinful heart may find some assuagement through the worship of these gilded, gaudy images. It is claimed by the priests and some of the more intelligent that the image worshiped is only a concrete representation of the saint, and it contains symbolically the spirit of the saint. To be sure! This is exactly the reason the more intelligent fetish worshiper in Africa assigns for worshiping his hand-made god. The etone or piece of wood is a representative of God and to a degree contains His spirit. Such worship is condemned as being idolatry in the African. The thing which is idolatry in the African must be idolatry in the Catholic. Even the Catholics will condemn the idol worship of the heathen, and yet this same Catholic church has in scores of places in South America and in other heathen lands, taken the identical images worshiped by the heathen and converted them into Catholic saints.

In the city of Braga, in Portugal, is a temple which centuries ago was devoted to Jupiter. It was afterward converted into a Catholic church and dedicated to St. Peter. The idol Jupiter, with two keys in his hand, was consecrated into St. Peter. In another part of the same city is a temple devoted to Janus in Roman times, which was turned into a temple dedicated to St. John. The idol which formerly was worshiped as Janus is being now worshiped as St. John. In the same temple there is an image now consecrated as St. Mark which was formerly the god Mars. The saint worship in Brazil is just as heathenish. In China Buddhist idols were renamed Jehosaphat by the Jesuits and worshiped. Their practices in Brazil are in keeping with their methods in other lands.

What is the difference between a worshiper who thus seeks indulgence through the worship of an image in Brazil and a like worshiper with a like soul need bowing before a similar wooden image in Africa or China?

CHAPTER VII

PENANCE AND PRIEST

Confession and penance play a large part in the religious life of the common people. The priests exercise great ingenuity to preserve the confessional. The better educated classes have long ago deserted the confessional, but it still holds sway over the common people and hangs like a dark shadow over the immoral deeds of the priests. Along with it flourishes the performance of penance. These two hand-maidens in wrong-doing often thrive in an absurd way.

In Penedo, the capital of the State of Alagoas, a new wharf was being built and the money granted by the Government was not sufficient to complete the work. The contractors approached the two monks who were to hold a mission in the city during February, 1904, and offered to pay them $500 if they would instruct the people to, in penance, carry across the city the stones which had been brought from the interior. A large quantity of building material had been brought down by rail and needed to be transported across to the wharf. The monks agreed, gave instructions accordingly, and in one week the people carried these stones across the town to the wharf. The transfer of these stones would have cost $2,500. At least 10,000 people engaged in this colossal act of penance. They came from two counties. Thus the contractors, by a little skillful manipulation, made penance save them considerable money.

In some of these penances the people wear crowns of thorns on their heads and cords about their necks and go barefooted through the streets of the city in their pilgrimages to the church. All, that through these means they may find some ease for the conscience which accuses them of evil.

What shall I say of the priests? I believe I will say nothing. I declined steadily to soil the pages of my note book with the records of the immoral deeds of these men. I will let speak for me an educated Brazilian, a teacher in an excellent school in Pernambuco, who is not a professing Christian, but who, like a great many of his class, admires Christianity very sincerely. When Mr. Colton, International Secretary of the Young Men's Christian Association, passed through Pernambuco in June, 1910, he was given a banquet by some of the leading men, which event offended so grievously the Catholic authorities that they published in the "Religious Tribune," their organ, a bitter diatribe on the Young Men's Christian Association. The professor, to whom I referred, who is now one of the leading judges in the state, published the following answer to this attack. He is in far better position to speak authoritatively about the Brazilian priests than I am. His article ran as follows:

"FURY UNBRIDLED."

"The official organ of the diocese of Olinda could not on this occasion control its great animus. It threw aside its old worn-out mantle of hypocrisy, it precipitated itself furiously and insolently against the Y.M.C.A. It not only does not forgive, but does not fear to excommunicate the local and State authorities who appeared at the banquet nor the directory of the Portuguese reading rooms who lent their hall to said Y.M.C.A.

"After affirming that the evangelization of Brazil means its unchristianizing the clerical organ begins to call the members of the Association and Protestants in general wolves in sheep's clothing.

"But we ask, to whom does this epithet apply better? To us who dress as the generality of men, thus leaving no doubt as to our sex and freeing our consciences from the ignominious Roman yoke, direct ourselves by that straight and narrow way which leads to salvation; or to this black band which secretly and maliciously makes of a man its prey from the moment in which he sees the light of day until the moment in which he goes to rest in the bosom of the earth? To us, Who having no thirst for dominion, seek to cultivate in man all the noble attributes given by the Creator, to us who teach clearly and without sophistry and gross superstitions the plan of salvation as it is found in the word of God; or to this legion of corrupt and hypocritical parasites, corruptors of youth, whose character they seek to debase and villify by means of the confessional?

"The only object of the wolf in dressing himself as a sheep is to devour the sheep. And these shaven heads know perfectly well why we cite the chronicles of the convents; they know from personal knowledge who are responsible for the greater part of the illegitimate children, and they have no doubt about the permanency and progress of prostitution.

"But they have effrontery, these priests!

"What has the priesthood done in Brazil in about 400 years? The answer is found in facts that prove the absence of all initiative of will, of strength, of energy and of activity. Brazil has only been a field for torpid exploitation by these gain-hunting libertines. And what of the attacks against private and public fortunes?

"Happily, for some years, the public conscience has been awakening and the people are beginning to know that a priest, even the best of them, is worthless.

"Freed from an official religion, the Brazilian people have really made progress in spite of the hopelessness of Romanism that perverts all things and resorts to ail sorts of schemes to preserve its former easy position

"We, pirates? Ah! deceivers. Then we, who present ourselves loyally without subterfuge, proclaiming the divine truths, speaking logically, without artifices or superstitions, are pirates? You noble priests are noble specimens of Christian culture, I must confess! You are such good things that France has already horsewhipped you out of the country, and Spain, whose knightly race is regaining the noble attributes obliterated by the iron yoke of Romanism, is about ready to apply to you the same punishment.

"There is no doubt that the priest is losing ground every day. All their manifestations of hate and satanic fury are easily explained.

"One easily recognizes the true value of the explosion of vicious egotism found in the official organ of the diocese of Olinda. The priest this time lost his calmness and let escape certain rude phrases as if he were yet in the good old times when he could imprison and burn at his pleasure. Console yourselves, reverend lord priests, everything comes to an end, and the ancient period of darkness and obscurity exists no more in Brazil."

What is the net result of such religious life as we have been portraying? The common and more ignorant people accept without very much questioning the teachings and practices which we have explained. The better educated people, especially the men, have lost confidence in the priesthood. Scarcely an educated man can be found who believes in the moral uprightness of the priest. The chief hold the Church has upon the better classes is a social and not a religious one. Births, marriages, deaths, alike are great social events, and upon such occasions, because it is custom to have a priest, the better classes of people even call in the services of the priests, in whom they have no confidence. The effect upon the beliefs of these better classes is most distressing. Spiritism, materialism and atheism are rampant, and one could well believe that these people set adrift without spiritual guides are in a worse condition than if they were still devout believers in the ancient practices of the Roman church. They are far more difficult to reach because they have imbibed the philosophies of spiritism, materialism and atheism. An atheist in South America is just as difficult to approach as he is anywhere. The devout Catholics are easier to reach with the gospel. The devout Catholic has at least one element which must always be reckoned with in dealing helpfully with an immortal soul. He has reverence, which thing many of those people who have been swung away from their faith have not. I take no comfort in the fact that the people in large numbers are deserting the Roman Catholic church and are being set adrift without any form of religion. One could wish that they might be held to their old beliefs until we could reach them with the virile truths of the gospel of Jesus.

We come back to it—the gospel is not preached in Brazil except as it is preached by the Protestant missionary. The need is just as great for gospel preaching in this country as it is in China.

One day after I had finished speaking to a congregation in Castello, back in the interior from Campos, an old English woman came up to me and expressed her great pleasure over having the privilege of hearing once more the gospel preached in English. I had spoken in English, and the missionary had interpreted what I had to say into Portuguese. She had heard the sermon twice. She had been in Brazil thirty-odd years. She and her husband had lived in the far interior. They had recently moved down to Castello that they might be near the little church where they could have the opportunity of worshiping God. She told me that back in the town in which they had lived they had left two sons who were engaged in business for themselves. These two sons had been born in Brazil, and yet in all their lives THEY HAD NEVER HEARD A GOSPEL SERMON. Yes, these people are without the gospel and this is our justification for carrying to them the message of life. For them Christ died, and to them, because they have not heard, He has sent us that we might bring His precious message of eternal salvation, for "How shall they believe in Him of whom they have not heard? And how shall they hear without a preacher?"

CHAPTER VIII

THE GOSPEL TRIUMPHANT

It is often claimed that the progress of the gospel is slower and more difficult in Catholic countries than in outright heathen lands. Such statements can be answered only by an appeal to the facts in the case. What are the facts? The Foreign Mission Board of the Southern Baptist Convention has been conducting operations in Brazil for about thirty years. It has been doing work in China for more than sixty years. During all the time since work—was opened in Brazil, the Board has had about three times as many missionaries in China as it had in Brazil, with the result that at the present time we have 9,939 members of our churches in Brazil, as against 9,990 members of our churches in China. We have worked less than half as long in Brazil and with one-third of the missionary force. Last year with a missionary force one-third as large in Brazil as it was in China, there were 635 more baptisms in Brazil than there were in China. There were 1,534 baptisms in China and 2,169 in Brazil. The same sort of comparison between our work in Italy and Japan would make the same showing. This is not to make a prejudicial statement concerning the work in any field. We make it simply to show that the gospel does succeed remarkably in the Catholic countries. The fact is, the rate of progress is far greater in the Catholic country than it is in the

Rev. T. B. Ray

heathen land. The gospel does succeed in Catholic countries. What is said here of the work of this one Board can he laid just as truly of the others.

It was our privilege to witness some remarkable demonstrations of the power of the gospel while we were in Brazil. About 3:30 o'clock one afternoon we arrived in Genipapo in the interior of the State of Bahia, after having ridden since early morning upon the railroad train through a mountainous country which, with its tropical vegetation, held our keenest interest. We were met at the station by some members of our church, who escorted us to the home of Polycarpo Nogueira. Mrs Nogueira is a very devout Christian. Some years ago she learned that her mother had embraced Christianity. Mrs. Nogueira set out upon a journey of 130 miles on muleback to her mother's home for the purpose of taking out of her mother's heart her belief in the gospel. She succeeded in shaking her mother's faith and also the faith of her brother. She now determined to prepare herself to combat this Baptist teaching which was spreading over the country. She marked passages of Scripture which she proposed to use against the Baptists. But when she used them she grew ashamed because she became conscious of the fact that she had misapplied the Word which she then gave deeper study. The Word of God took hold of her own heart and she in turn was converted. Her first thought was concerning her mother and brother 130 miles away. Again she took the long journey on muleback in order to lead her loved ones to Christ. She was able to re-establish her mother's faith, but to this day her deep regret is that her brother does not believe.

We had a great service at the church that night. The crowd was so large that we held the services out in the open. Seven stood to confess their surrender to Christ. The good deacon of the church was so thoroughly in the spirit of the occasion and in such sympathy with me that he declared he could understand my English. He really seemed to catch it before the missionary could interpret it.

On the following day we reached St. Inez, the station at the end of the railway, and spent the night in a poor excuse of a lodging house called the Commercial Hotel.

At 7 o'clock on the following morning, which was Sunday, we started on horseback for Arroz Novo, an excellent country church fifteen miles away. A young brother named John Laringeiro (John Orangetree) had brought horses for us. Before his conversion he was an arch persecutor, and since he has become a Christian he has been called upon to suffer even more bitter persecution than he ever inflicted upon others. He is struggling to care for his mother, and as the pastor of the church at Rio Preto, he is a most acceptable gospel preacher.

It was a fine ride into the country, over hill and mountain and deeply-shaded valley. After we had ridden about half the length of our journey several brethren from Arroz Novo (New Rice) met us to escort us to the church. A mile or two further we were met by another company, who swelled the number of our dashing cavalcade to about twenty-five. It was dashing, too, for they were hard riders. It was a very joyous and cordial reception committee. Finally we rode into sight of the church, winch is located on a high hill commanding a grand panorama of the mountains. As we approached we saw two long lines of people standing facing each other in front of the church. The men were on one side and the women on the other—about 600 of them. As we rode up the congregation sang a hymn to give us welcome. We dismounted when we reached the end of the two lines and walked down between them to the church. Now it is the custom in Brazil upon festal occasions to strew the meeting place with oleander and cinnamon leaves and to throw rose petals and confetti upon those they wish to honor. These good people observed this custom generously that day. A wide space of the ground in front of the church was strewed with leaves, and they showered such quantities of rose petals and confetti upon us that we were beautiful sights by the time we reached the door.

We entered the very creditable church building into which the people now poured until every foot of space was occupied. There was hardly room left for me to make gestures as I spoke. It was ten o'clock. The people had been present since four engaged in a prayer meeting. We began the service immediately. The Spirit of the Lord was upon us to preach the gospel. Afterward we called for those who wished to make confession of their faith in Christ. We pushed back the people a little bit in the front and the space thus made vacant was immediately filled with those who wished to confess their Lord and Savior. We saw that others wanted to come, so we asked them to stand where they were. All through the audience they rose. Then began the examination of these candidates. Numerous questions were put to them by the missionary and the pastor of the church. Sometimes as many as twenty-five or even more questions would be asked an individual so great was the care exercised in examining those who wished to become members of the church, and what impressed me most was the fact that after every question they could think of had been asked, they would ask if anyone present could endorse him. Whereupon someone, if he could recommend the candidate would, after a brief speech of endorsement, make a motion to receive him.

Over to my right rose a young woman who was the most beautiful woman I saw in Brazil. Her name was Elvira Leal. She had been favorable to the gospel for some time and had suffered cruel persecution from her father. The tears streamed down her face as she spoke, saying, "You know my story and what I have been called upon to endure for the gospel's sake, but this morning I must confess the Lord. I cannot resist the Spirit longer." I learned that her father, in order to force her to give up her faith, had dragged her across the floor by her hair. He had brandished his dagger over her heart, threatening to take her life; he had forced her to break her engagement to be married to the young preacher, John Larinjeiro, who had brought the horses for us; he had declared he would kill both of them rather than to allow them to marry, and at the time we were there she was compelled to live in the home of a neighbor, so violent had become her father in his opposition to her adherence to the gospel. That morning, however, she said though she knew it involved suffering, she would follow her Savior at whatever cost.

By the time the missionary had finished examining this woman, a man had crowded near to the front and indicated that he wished to say something. It was John Larinjeiro's brother. He said that for two years he had been impressed with the gospel, but because of the persecution in his own home he had held back. When years ago his mother had been converted, he went to persuade her to give up her religion. Persuasion failing, he persecuted her severely. She finally told him that his efforts were of no avail because she could not give up her faith in Christ, yet if he would take the Bible and show her where she was wrong, she would give it up. He secured a gospel circulated by the priest and also "The Manual of Instructions for Holding Missions" and both of these confirmted his mother's faith, and he had no more to say. The Word impressed itself upon his heart and he became sympathetic to the gospel. Then trouble arose. His father-in-law, he said, had threatened to take his wife and children from him and to put him out of his own home. His wife had persecuted him and declared she would leave him if he made the confession he desired to make. He said that he did not know what to do, but had come forward to ask us to pray for him. Then the congregation fell upon its face, as far as such a thing was possible, and prayed. I could not understand all they said in the prayers because they were spoken in Portuguese, but so mighty was the presence of the Spirit and so irresistible was the appeal sent up to the throne of Grace that I knew before the prayers ended what the result would be. As soon as the prayers were concluded, the man stood up and said, "News travels quickly in this country. It may be that when I reach home I shall find my wife and children gone, but whatever may he the cost, I cannot resist the Spirit today. I must confess my Lord and ask for membership in the church." Of course, he was received. A letter received from the missionary some months later informed me that the father-in-law had carried out his threat and did take away the wife and children.

Numerous others stood to make confession, and the examination continued far past one o'clock, 'till twenty-one were received for baptism. This marvelous outpouring of the Spirit of Christ enabled us to see with our own eyes the power of the gospel demonstrated in the saving of souls in Brazil.

After the service we went to breakfast in a house near by. The crowd, according to custom, came into the dining room, as many of them as could, to hear the conversation while we sat about the table. The walls of the building were made of mud, the floor was the bare ground, in the corner of the room, surrounded by a mud puddle, stood a water jar, around which the chickens were picking. I kicked a pig out of my way, accidentally stepped on a dog, but nothing daunted, fell to with good will and ate, asking no questions.

After a few hours' ride, upon our return journey in the afternoon, we reached the town of Olhos d'Agua (Fountains of Water) through which we had passed upon our outward journey in the early morning. There is a very good church at this place which has suffered cruel persecution. Upon the doors of every Protestant house in the town have been painted black crosses. They were placed there at night by the Catholics to keep the Devil from coming out. The black cross of derision has become a mark of honor in that community. We were greeted by a splendid audience that night and the gospel again was honored. More than a dozen people accepted Christ and made confession of Him.

I was greatly interested in Brother Raymundo, who is the leading member of this church. Formerly he was a great persecutor. He was an enemy to Antonio Barros, who is now a leading member in the church at Arroz Novo. Barros was converted at Lage, and when he met Raymundo he greeted him, at which Raymundo was greatly surprised. Barros explained his action by saying that he had found Christ and wanted to live at peace with all men. The fact that his enemy should embrace him and beg his pardon greatly impressed Raymundo. Upon the invitation of Barros, Raymundo attended the meeting that night. He was touched by the gospel and was converted. He now had to experience the same persecution he had inflicted upon others. His enemies wrote to the merchants in Bahia and told them that he was out of his mind. So persistent was their persecution that he was compelled to give up his business. His credit was destroyed by these reports. He moved away from Olhos d'Agua, but when the native pastor left the place recently Raymundo returned in order to hold the work together. He now makes his meager living by trading, and through great sacrifice leads the congregation in a very acceptable service.

We returned to St. Ignez by ten o'clock that night, tired and happy over what our eyes had seen and our hearts had felt. It had been a day of triumph for the gospel.

Rev. T. B. Ray

On Monday we started on our journey for Santo Antonio. When we passed through Genipapo we found Brother Polycarpo Nogueira at the station. He had come to ask about a passage of Scripture I had pointed out to him on the night when we stayed in his home We had urged him to accept the gospel and he hesitated. I quoted to him, "Everyone, therefore, who shall confess me before men, him will I confess before my Father in Heaven. But whosoever shall deny me before men, him, will I deny before my Father who is in Heaven." Mat. 10:32, 33. He told us about a wonderful meeting held in the church on Sunday, in which one had been converted and many others were deeply interested. He himself was evidently moved upon by the Spirit. May the word we gave him lead him to Christ.

Some hours further on we passed through Vargem Grande, where we have another church. Several people boarded the train to accompany us to Santo Antonio. One of them was Fausto de Almeida. When the ex-priest, Ottoni, visited Vargem Guande some years ago to preach the gospel this man Almeida, with a great crowd of boys equipped with tin cans, mct him at the station. This troupe escorted Ottoni to the church and stood outside making as much noise as possible. He offered the ex-priest a loaded cigar, which Ottoni declined with kindly thanks. The minister's conduct was so gentle and kind that Fausto, when he bethought himself, went home in a rage, became intoxicated, and in order to vent his wrath, went out into his back yard and fired his pistols. A little later one of his sisters was converted, and by her good testimony not long after that when she died, he was greatly impressed. Another sister was converted and gave him a Bible, which he read and in which he found the message of Christ. He obeyed his Lord, and in spite of violent opposition on the part of his wife, is today in a faithful and effective way, building up the church at Vargem, Grande.

CHAPTER IX

JOSE BARRETTO

When we reached Santo Antonio de Jesus at two p. m. we found a throng at the station to meet us. They gave us a royal welcome, receiving us literally with open arms. After this hearty greeting we formed a procession and marched two and two through the streets of the city to the church. They wished us to take the lead in the procession, but we declined the honor and finally took position about the middle of the line. They seemed to march through every street in the city, so eager were they to impress the population that there was somebody else in the world besides their religious persecutors. When we arrived at the church they showered us once more with rose petals and confetti. After prayer we were taken to the home of Jose Barretto to be entertained.

Now, this same Jose Barretto is a very remarkable character. He was formerly Superintendent of the Manganese mines near by and very active in politics. If any questionable work needed to be done in order to influence an election Jose was called upon to do it. He is a great, strong fellow, more than six feet in height and weighs, perhaps, 250 pounds. He was a violent man, fearless and desperate. I noted many scars on his face which were evidences of many dangerous encounters. He did not deign to steal the ballots, but would take possession of the ballot box, extract from it the proper number of votes, destroy them, seal the box and allow the count to be made. No one dared withstand him. He was just as violent in his opposition to the Protestants. He declared that he would beat any Protestant who should ever come into his house.

Well, one day his own brother-in-law came to see him. This brother-in-law was blind and also a Christian. After a while Jose and his wife were commiserating the brother over his blindness when he said, that though his eyes were clouded, his soul saw the light of life. His sister said to him, "You must be a Protestant." He replied, "Yes, thank God, I know Jesus Christ." She was so frightened that she fainted, because she had visions of her burly husband pouncing upon her blind brother and beating him to death. Her husband resuscitated her and soothed her by saying, "I know I have said all of these things about what I would do to the Protestants, but I hope I am not mean enough to strike a blind man and certainly I would not injure your brother." That night the brother asked them to read the Scriptures. They had no Bible, but did possess a book of Bible stories, one of which the sister read, and then the brother asked permission to pray. Jose Barretto had always been reverential, and so he knelt in prayer. So earnest and childlike was the praying of the blind brother and so fully did he express the real heart hunger of the great, strong man that when the prayer was finished, Jose Barretto said very sincerely, "Amen." He became deeply interested in the gospel.

When the brother left, the Spirit of God so impressed Jose that he felt he must look up a New Testament which he had taken from an employee some time ago. He had looked at this book which he had taken from the employee's hands, and finding no saints' pictures in it, concluded that it was that hated Protestant Bible the priests were trying to keep from being circulated, and had thrown it into a box in the corner of his office. Now he went to this box, fished out the New Testament, brushed the dust from its pages and read from it the word of life. The blind brother, in the meantime, had gone to Santo Antonio and told what had happened. The chief of police of the city, who was a Christian and the President of the Baptist Young People's Union, declared that he was going out to see Jose. "I have been afraid to go," he said, "because Jose has been so violently opposed to the gospel."

He went and found the strong man poring over the pages of the book in his effort to find the way of life. He explained the gospel and Barretto was soon converted, as was also his sister. His wife held on to her old faith. She would pray, but would use the Crucifix. Finally the husband and sister decided they would burn the idol, which they accordingly did. When the wife saw that no dreadful calamity befell the house she concluded that the idol was a powerless thing and gave her heart to Christ.

The life of Jose Barretto since that time has been a burning light. He has been as zealous in following Christ as he ever was in following evil, though not so violent. His witness has been honored amongst his own family and relations especially. They have been forced to realize that there is something in Christianity which can produce such a remarkable change in the life of such a violent man. When we were in his home we learned of a family of twenty-one, some distance out in the country, who were ready to make confession of their faith and be baptized. They were anxious for the missionary to come and baptize them and to organize a church in one of their homes. These people were the relatives of Jose Barretto. It is marvelous how the witness of his life is bearing fruit. He lost his position as Superintendent by his acceptance of Christ, but is now making a living as a coffee merchant.

We had a remarkable service at the church that night. A great throng pressed into the building, and Jose Barretto was the chief usher. I have never seen a man who could crowd more people into a building than could he. After the house had been packed there still remained on the outside a crowd as large as that sandwiched into the building. I preached the gospel once more, speaking, of course, in all of these services through an interpreter. When I called for those who would confess Christ I did not ask them to come forward because there was no room for them. They stood here and there over the audience until more than twenty expressed themselves as having accepted Christ and desiring membership in the church. When one man stood amongst this number I noticed that Jose Barretto was very deeply moved. His great frame shook with emotion. I learned afterwards that the man who stood was a police sergeant, who in the old days had been Jose's confederate in his political crookedness. That night this man stood acknowledging his sins and asking for membership in the church. Jose's faithfulness had won him. Once more we witnessed a marvelous victory of the gospel.

On the very day on which we visited Santo Antonio and were entertained in the home of our good brother Jose Barretto, this great stalwart fellow who had been such a violent opposer of Christianity and who had previously lived such a desperate life, was met on the street by one of his former schoolmates. His schoolmate chided him for becoming a Christian and insinuated that Jose's conversion was an act of weakness and also that he would not hold out very long. He went further to say many severe things in criticism of the cause of Protestant Christianity. Jose Barretto replied, "You ought to be ashamed of yourself for finding fault with the thing which has produced such a change in my life. You know the kind of character I have been in this community. You know how violent and sinful I have been and you know at this time how I am living. A religion which can produce such a change as this does not deserve ridicule." The man turned and slunk away. In the meantime, there had gathered around them a number of people, because they knew how serious a matter it was for anyone to oppose him, and they expected to see something violent take place that day. Being emboldened by the mild answer which he gave to his persecutor, others began to ask questions. Finally one of them asked him this question: "Suppose someone should strike you in the face in persecution, what would you do?" And then the great, strong violent man who had been made meek and humble by his acceptance of Jesus gave an answer which showed him to be genuinely converted to the Spirit of Jesus. He said: "I am not afraid of such a thing as that happening, for the reason that I propose to live in this community such a life for the help of my brothers that no one will ever desire to strike me in the face," and these others turned shame-stricken away from him. He threw down before that community the challenge of his life, and that is the thing that not only in Brazil, but here in our own land, must finally win for our King the triumph which is His due.

CHAPTER X

CAPTAIN EGYDIO

What brought about the readiness of this territory in the interior of the State of Bahia for the acceptance of the gospel? Perhaps the brand of burning which did more than any other to shed light through the entire section over which we passed, was the person of Captain Egydio Pereira de Almeida. He was one of several brothers of a good country family which owned large possessions in the interior 150 miles from the city of Bahia. He was an intense Catholic, but never a persecutor. At one time he was Captain in the National Guards. He was political boss of his community and protector for a small tribe of Indians. He was a hard-working, law-abiding citizen.

In order to know the story we must go back a little. In 1892 Solomon Ginsburg sold a Bible to Guilhermino de Almeida on the train when he was going to Armagoza. Ginsburg had only one Bible left and felt constrained to offer it to the stranger across the aisle. The man said he had no money and did not care to buy. The missionary pressed him and finally sold him for fifty cents a Bible worth four times that amount. That night his fellow passenger heard the missionary speak in the theater in Armagoza and seemed to enjoy especially the hymns the preacher sang. The missionary marked for him the Ten Commandments and other passages in the Bible.

When the man reached his home at Vargem Grande a few days afterward he told his brother Marciano de Almeida of his encounter with the missionary, of how he had bought the Bible which he did not want and of the Ten Commandments the missionary had marked for him. He very willingly gave his Bible to his brother. Marciano read the book and was particularly impressed with the Ten Commandments.

Now, we must introduce into this narrative another character in the person of good Brother Madeiros. Some time before this, having become interested in the gospel, he had gone to Bahia and had been instructed by Missionary Z. C. Taylor in the truth to such good purpose that he gave himself to the Lord. His neighbors at Valenca, his native town, on learning of his having accepted Christ, drove him out, and he moved to Vargem Grande. But he found no rest in his new home, for his fellow townsmen so persecuted him that he was compelled to live in the outskirts of the town. He was the first believer in Vargem Grande. When Marciano de Almeida became interested in the Scriptures he went to see Madeiros and was instructed by him in the gospel. He told the persecuted saint that he would stand by him from now on, for Marciano had experienced a marvelous conversion.

On learning that his images were idols, Marciano collected all immediately and burnt them, greatly to the disgust of his family and the whole town. He began at once to declare the Word of God, and though he was as gentle as a lamb, he was also as bold as a lion in defending the gospel.

When his brother, Captain Egydio de Almeida, who lived sixty miles away, learned that Marciano had become converted, he made the journey to take out of his brother's heart the false teaching which he had imbibed. He pitied his brother, thinking that Marciano's mind had become unbalanced. When Captain Egydio arrived at his brother's in Vargem Grande, being a very positive man, he set about the business of straightening out his brother with dispatch and determination. He failed in his purpose, and then called in a priest. When he returned with the priest Marciano asked the two to be seated. Immediately the priest inquired, "What is this I am hearing about you, Marciano?" He replied, "Mr. Priest, I am thirty-five years old and you never gave me the Bible, God's Holy Law and as God ordered it. I came by it through the Protestants whom you have always abused. You have taken my money all these years for mass, saying you would take the souls of our kin out of a purgatory that does not exist. You taught me to worship idols which God's Word condemns. You sprinkle my children for money, marry them for money, and when they die you still demand money to save their souls from an imaginary purgatory. The Bible teaches me, on the other hand, that God offers me a free salvation through Jesus Christ." The priest rose and said good-bye without offering a word of explanation. Seeing the priest thus defeated, Captain Egydio turned to old Brother Madeiros, who happened to be present, and said: "If you continue to put these false doctrines in my brother's head I will send a couple of Indians here to take off your head." "Yes," replied Madeiros, "you may cut off my head, but you cannot cut off my soul from God." Captain Egydio returned home breathing out plagues upon himself and his family. He drank heavily at every grog shop on his way and scattered abroad the news about his family's disgrace. He was a man of a kind heart, and though he did not embrace the truths of his brother's religion, he did show his brother great consideration and, being a political leader for that district, became his brother's protector.

When his wrath had cooled down somewhat he began to recall many things Marciano had told him about the Bible, and as he looked upon his many expensive idols set here and there in niches about his home, he said to himself: "Well, did Marciano say these images do nothing. They neither draw water, cut wood nor pick coffee. They do not teach school, they do not protect our home, for there is one covered with soot. There is another the rats have gnawed, and recently another fell and was broken. How powerless they are." Then he remembered the Bible which a believer had given him years before. He began to examine it in a closed room. Ag he read he prayed, "Oh, God, if this religion of Marciano be right, show it to me."

He seemed to be making good progress. But about this time he received word that his brother and the missionary R. E Neighbor were coming to see him. The priest had also heard of the approaching visit and had sent a letter to Captain Egydio's son warning him against the coming men, saying that they were emissaries of the United States and wished to lead the Almeidas astray. The letter bearer was instructed to deliver the letter to the son and not let the father know anything about it, but he said, "I cannot do that because I must be true to my old captain," so he gave the letter to Captain Egydio. He wag greatly disturbed over the warnings the priest had given and tried to induce his children to give up the reading of the pamphlets and Scriptures he had given to them, which thing they refused to do.

His brother and the missionary came according to agreement and Captain Egydio, true to his word, went with them to the town of Areia to protect them while they were engaged in conducting a gospel service in the public square. The priest of the town sent the police to prevent the Protestants from conducting the meeting. The sergeant, who had been under Captain Egydio when he was Captain in the National Guards, was one of the detail sent to suppress the meeting. He declared that he would stand by his old Captain, for the men knew that under the Constitution the missionary had a perfect right to hold the meeting. The meeting was held, but under such unfavorable circumstances that the Captain stood forth and said: "I have not declared myself a Protestant, but from this time I shall be a Protestant and propose to give my life to the spread of this faith."

It happened that one day he was called to visit a boy who had been shot. As he rode along through the open fields he was burdened with prayer to God. Suddenly he felt a strange feeling and he seemed to hear a voice saying, "You are saved." Immediately he knew that the Lord had visited him with His blessed salvation. He shouted as he rode along the way, "Glory to God. I am redeemed." He rode on in this state to the home of the boy. Seeing the boy could not live, he began to exhort him to look to Christ for salvation, and just before the boy's spirit passed out from him, he made confession of his Lord. The Captain returned to his home overflowing with joy. He galloped his horse up to the door, shouting, "Glory, hallelujah, I am saved." He embraced his wife and children and all stood back staring at him. Finally the mother cried: "Poor man! Children, your father is mad. Get the scissors and let us cut off his hair; let us rub some liniment on his head." "All right," he said, "only do not cut it too close," and he suffered them to rub the liniment also upon his head. Seeing that there was no change in him, they also administered to him one of their homely medicines, a small portion of which he was willing to take to pacify them. Their opinion of his sanity was not changed.

Not only his family, but his neighbors suspected him. As he engaged in business—and he was a very busy man—people were watching him to see if something was not dreadfully wrong. Finally all realized that a great and beneficent change had taken place. He never became a preacher, but he did not allow to pass an opportunity to tell the story of his newly-found Savior. His Bible was constantly in his hands, and he read the marvelous news to all. His family soon became interested in the gospel and they, even to his son-in-law, became as crazy upon the subject as he. Thirteen of them were baptized at one time.

For activity in evangelization his equal was scarcely ever met. He kept for distribution boxes of Bibles and tracts. While at business he witnessed for the gospel. He traveled extensively. Some of his bosom friends became his worst enemies, but many of them he led to Christ, or at least to a friendship, for the gospel. He did not preach, but invited many preachers to come to his community and was always ready to accompany them whenever they needed his presence. His life was the greatest sermon he could preach to the people. They had known him once in the old days when one of his sons fell sick he promised to carry his weight of beeswax to the miracle working saint of the Lapa shrine, 100 miles away on the San Francisco River. The son recovered and the father kept his word. Now they saw him discard his old superstitions for the truth in Jesus. The gospel that could produce such a marvelous change as this had its effect upon his neighbors. He organized a church upon his own fazenda and it held its meetings in his own house at Casca.

He became deeply interested in the subject of education. He said one day to Dr. Z. C. Taylor, our missionary at Bahia: "While I was a Catholic I had no desire to educate my children, but now I would give all of this farm to see them educated. Dr. Taylor told him of some of his own plans concerning a school, and Captain Egydio contributed the first money for the school, which Dr. Taylor afterward established, Captain Egydio's gift of a thousand dollars making it possible for this school to be organized.

Of the trials and persecutions which he endured for the

gospel, we can cite only one or two.

A priest paid two men sixty dollars to go and take the Captain's life. They appeared one night at his door and asked for employment. He invited them in, saying he had plenty of work he could give them to do. The time soon arrived for family prayers and the men were invited to be present. The Captain afterward told the family that while he was praying he received a distinct impression that the men had come to do him bodily injury and that in the prayer he had committed himself absolutely to the protection of God. The next day he took the two men out into the field to show them what to do. In the meantime he had been telling them of the love of Jesus and how He had come to save to the uttermost those who would believe on Him. One lingered behind to shoot, but his hand trembled too much. The other did not have the courage to do the man of God any injury. That night they said they would not stay longer. He paid them for the day's work, bade them godspeed and they departed.

But he did not always escape suffering so easily. One afternoon as he was passing by the priest's home the priest accosted him and said: "Captain, why is it you do not stop with me any more? You used to do so, but of late you have passed me by." He urged the Captain so strongly that he decided to stay all night. They offered him wine to drink, which he refused. Then they gave him coffee. That night he suffered agony and was sick for some time after reaching home. He was sure he had been poisoned.

He suffered many persecutions from unsympathetic neighbors, not only from criticism, but sometimes from bodily injuries and from painful abuse, all of which he bore with an equanimity of spirit which would do credit to any martyr to the cause of Christ.

Dr. Z. C. Taylor relates a trying experience through which he and Captain Egydio passed together.

"The Captain and I were together one day returning home from a preaching tour by a near cut, passing the door of our greatest persecutor, Captain Bernadino, who on seeing us, seized a stick, and running to us, beat back our hordes, crying, 'Back, back, you cannot pass my house.' A plunge of my horse caused my hat to fall off, which he handed me and continued to force our retreat. We returned by way of the home of his son-in-law, who was a baptized believer, and while this brother was piloting us down a hill to another way home Captain Bernadino, jumping from behind a bush, caught my horse by the bridle. He had an assassin at his heels, with axe in hand, asking every minute what he should do. Captain Bernadino wore out his stick on my horse, planting the last stroke across my loins; then he struck me about a dozen times in the breast with his fist. I said to him, 'Captain, why are you beating me, I believe in God; do not you also?' Stopping and panting he said, 'Do you believe in God, you rascal?' 'Yes,' I said, 'and Jesus also who came to save us sinners.' 'Don't let up, don't let up, hit him, hit him,' cried his wife and children. He pulled the bridle from my hands, led my horse into a pond close by, and gathering mud, pelted me from foot to shoulder. Then leaving my horse, he went after Captain Egydio, who was guarded by another assassin. On passing his son-in-law, kneeling, he struck him on the head, saying, 'Get up, you fool!' Leading the Captain's horse into the water, he covered him with mud from foot to head. Then, putting our bridles up, he beat our horses and told us to go, never to be seen in those parts any more. My bridle reins he crossed, which fact caused me when I passed his wife, who stood with a long stick upraised, to strike me, to turn my horse upon her instead of away from her, and the horse came near running over her. She struck and fell back, the stick falling across my horse's neck. Such a pandemonium of mad voices, cursing and shouting as we left I never heard. It took us till night to reach home. The family took it as an honor, and smiling and laughing, we were spending the evening merrily, when at nine or ten o'clock a rap at the door caused us all to suspend our hilarity. It was that son- in-law of the persecutor, bringing his wife, asking to be baptized. She had witnessed the persecution her father gave us, and on her husband's return to the house, she told him the scene made her think of the Apostles and that now she was determined to be baptized. At first I thought of bloodshed, for her father had threatened to kill her, her mother, Captain Egydio and the man who baptized her. But I had always taught them to obey Christ and leave results with Him, so we heard her experience and at midnight I baptized her.

Captain Egydio did not complain of our treatment nor did I ever mention it to our Consul.

When he gave his heart to Christ he gave his life and all. He followed where his conscience led. Before his conversion he was a great smoker. The missionary asked him one day if he smoked for the glory of God. He took the cigarette from his mouth, threw it away and never smoked again. This was characteristic of his determination and his unfaltering devotion to what he esteemed to be right.

The end came swiftly one night. He had an attack apparently of indigestion which carried him speedily away. The symptoms seemed to indicate that he had been poisoned. All that night he spent in prayer and in singing hymns. He died leaving his benediction upon his family and upon those Brazilians who would give their hearts and their services to Jesus Christ.

He was buried upon his own farm. As his family did not

erect a cross over his grave, one of his neighbors who had persecuted Captain Egydio violently many times thought he would correct him in his grave, and so he set up a large cross over him. One night soon after, this cross was cut down. The violent neighbor instituted a suit for the violation of the law in tearing down a symbol of the Roman Catholic church. He also came with great pomp, accompanied by soldiers, and set up another cross. The law suit finally wore itself out and both parties were glad to drop it, each party sharing an equal amount of the costs.

The persecution has been so bitter that the church which Captain Egydio organized in his own house was removed to Pe da Serra, three miles away, and from there it was driven by persecution to Rio Preto, where today it flourishes with a membership of about fifty people and is in a hopeful condition. The widow and her children have been compelled to move into the city of Bahia. A recent letter informs me of the conversion of the two youngest girls.

The witness of Captain Egydio has not been lost. It is marvelous how much he accomplished in his short career. He was converted October, 1894, baptized February 4, 1895, and died March 30th, 1898, at fifty years of age. In these few years he sowed the country down with the gospel truth. We visited Vargem Grande, Santo Antonio, Areia and Genipapo churches, all of which had grown very largely out of the influence of this one man, and had we been permitted to go further, we might have visited several other churches for whose beginning the life of this valiant servant of God was in a great measure responsible. "He, being dead, yet speaketh."

Rev. T. B. Ray

CHAPTER XI

FELICIDADE

One of the most fascinating phases of mission study is the tracing of the lines along which the gospel spreads. This is true because it brings us into touch with the native Christian who is one of the greatest agencies for the spread of the gospel. As it was in the first century, so it is now—"they that were scattered abroad went everywhere preaching the gospel." The history of those Apostolic times repeats itself in every mission land. He who personally observes the work in Brazil or any other mission field will have a keener appreciation and understanding of the Acts of the Apostles written by Luke. The native Christians must either witness for their Lord or else betray Him. There is no middle ground. A large percentage of the churches in Brazil grew out of the fact that a believer moved into a community and began to tell the story of the love of Jesus to his neighbors. He may have entered this community by choice or may have been driven into it by persecution. However, that may be, the truth is that many a poor, despised, often persecuted believer, has started a movement in a community which gathered to itself a large company of believers, and formed the nucleus of another one of those most wonderful institutions in all the world—a church of Jesus Christ.

When I had entered the First Baptist Church in Sao Paulo, Brazil, and stood for a moment looking about me, I heard someone exclaim, "Oh, there he is! There he is!" and presently I found myself locked in the affectionate embrace of an apparently very happy old woman. She was about seventy years of age. She was the janitress of the church. She had looked forward to our coming with joyful pleasure, and gave to us as hearty a welcome as did anyone in Brazil. Her name was Felicidade, which being translated means "Felicity."

Several years ago she had come from Pernambuco, in which city and State she had labored with great success for many years in behalf of the gospel.

When a girl of ten or twelve years of age she heard her father talk about a book he had seen in the court-house upon which the Judge had laid his hand as he administered the oath. She had the greatest desire to see this book. She was married in her thirteenth year and her husband died when she was eighteen. After his death she went from the country to the city of Pernambuco, where she met some members of the Congregational Church and was led by them to attend the services. She saw the Bible and heard a sermon preached from the text, "Blessed are they that hunger and thirst," and soon afterward she gave obedience to Jesus.

From that time forth her whole conversation was upon the gospel and upon the subject of bringing other people to Christ. One time when Mrs. Entzminger was away from the city of Pernambuco she left her children in charge of Felicidade. While Felicidade was passing along the street with the children one day she was met by Mrs. Maria Motta and her daughter, who stopped to admire the beautiful children. Felicidade told who the children were and urged her new acquaintances to attend the church services. They accepted her invitation and soon became interested in the gospel, and before long were converted to faith in Jesus Christ.

Then their persecution began. They lost all their friends and endured many other hardships. They came from one of the best families in the city, and therefore felt the persecution more bitterly than might have some others. The girl, Augusta, secured work in the English store. Her mother took in fine ironing, and thus the two made their support. Afterward Augusta married Augusto Santiago, who at the present time is the pastor of our thriving church in the city of Nazareth. She has been to him one of the greatest blessings in that she has done much to help him in his effort to prepare himself better for his work. When we visited Nazareth we were entertained in the delightful home of Augusto Santiago and found it to be charming in every respect.

When Felicidade lived in Pernambuco it was her custom to sell fruit for six months to make money enough to live upon for the remainder of the year. She would then go into the interior with tracts and Bibles, sell them and in every way try to lead people to Christ. One year she made it her aim to lead not less than twelve to her Lord, and she was able to accomplish her purpose. Her education is limited, but she knows any number of Scripture verses, which she is able to quote with remarkable aptness.

Upon one of her visits into the interior she was found at Nazareth by Innocencio Barbosa, a farmer who resided in the district of Ilheitas. He lived about thirty miles from Nazareth. He took Felicidade home with him in order that she might teach the gospel to his family. Meanwhile, his friend, Hermenigildo, who lived in a distant neighborhood, bought a Bible in Limoeiro and told his friend Innocencio of what he had done. Innocencio told him of the presence of Felicidade and suggested that his friend might take her home with him that she might explain the gospel to his family also. Felicidade accordingly went into this other home and soon the entire family, including a son-in-law and some relatives, were led to Jesus, and a church of about fifty members was organized in Hermenigildo's house.

Thus the faithful witnessing of this humble, consecrated woman was so honored of the Holy Spirit that scores were led into the light of the gospel of Jesus. Out of her efforts grew churches which the violence of the oppressor could not destroy, because the work she did became immortal when it passed over into the hands of the Lord of Hosts, against whose church not even the gates of Hell can prevail.

Rev. T. B. Ray

CHAPTER XII

PERSECUTION

Some of the severest persecutions the saints have ever endured in Pernambuco broke upon this new congregation in the Ilheitas district. The houses of the believers were broken into and everything destroyed, some of the buildings were burned. The believers asked for police protection, but the police sent to protect them being under the domination of the priest, who was the political boss of that district, persecuted the believers even more than their neighbors had done. They drove the believers about, beating them with their swords, forcing them to drink whisky and in many ingenious ways heaped indignities upon them. After the success of the great persecution in Bom Jardim, of which we will speak later, the priest organized a large force of men to destroy everything belonging to the Protestants in the Ilheitas district and to drive them away. They burned all of the church furniture, as well as the household furniture belonging to Hermenigildo, who was forced to flee for his life. They cut the cord to the hammock in which was lying his young baby. The fall broke the neck of the child. The mother was driven unclothed between two lines of soldiers and severely beaten. The other believers were so harrassed that most of them were compelled to leave the neighborhood. Hermenigildo stayed away five months, when a change in police chiefs in

Pernambuco made it possible for him to return. The church was reorganized the following year. A new building was constructed on Hermenigildo's farm and today, with a membership of 103, it is in a most prosperous condition.

In the little city of Nazareth the fury of persecution has been felt. Not a great while after the church had been organized by Dr. Entzminger the farmers in the community and the priest combined to drive the Protestants out of town. Dr. Entzminger heard of their purpose and went up to Nazareth, accompanied by a number of soldiers whom the Government had put at his disposal. A great throng was collected at the station to do violence to the missionary on his arrival, but when they saw the soldiers they took to their heels, and many came that night to the service to show that they were not in the mob. A year or two later another mob broke into the church, poured oil over the furniture and burned practically everything. The police saved the building. Once after this, when Missionary Ginsburg was to hold an open-air meeting in this same town, a soldier was hired to take his life. The officers of the law left town in order that the deed might be done without hindrance. The soldier drank whisky in order to brace himself for the deed, and fortunately imbibed too much and became so intoxicated that he fell asleep. When he awoke the meeting had been held and he had missed his chance. These facts were confessed by the soldier to Dr. Entzminger after the soldier had been converted a year later.

At the railway station at Nazareth we met Primo da Fonseca, who had, for the sake of the gospel, lost all in a great persecution at Bom Jardim, which is not a great distance from Nazareth. He was a reader of evangelical literature and preached the gospel all over that country, though he had not been baptized. A native missionary went into that region, began preaching and soon afterward gathered a congregation and organized a church in Fonseca's home. The political boss of the community planned with the Catholics to take 800 men into Bom Jardim on the night of April 15th, 1900, for the purpose of killing all the Protestants who were in prayer at Fonseca's house. The mob divided into two parties. One party was to approach the house from the front and the other from the opposite side. A gun was to be fired as a signal for the attack. The first party approached the house, which was near the theater. Now in the theater at that time was gathered a great throng of people. When the news came to them of the approach of the mob the women thought it was a part of the band of bandits led by Antonio Silvino, who is perhaps the most famous outlaw of Brazil. All were greatly frightened. The Mayor went out to see if he could not do something to persuade the mob to leave the town. After some parleying they said that inasmuch as the Mayor asks, we will turn back. Someone at that time fired a shot and shouted, "Viva Santa Anna" in honor of the patron saint of that city. This signal brought up the supporting party at once, who mistook their comrades for the believers and fired into them. In the melee twenty people were killed and about fifty wounded. All night they were carrying the dead away to burial in order that they might cover up the deed as far as possible. The Municipal Judge made out a case that the Protestants had fired on the Catholics. He pronounced nineteen as being implicated. Several escaped, six were finally brought to trial. Dr. Entzminger in Pernambuco sent lawyers and gave such assistance as he could. After about two years, Missionary Ginsburg having come also to help in the meantime, the men on trial were set free. Fonseca lost all he had in this law suit, he being one of those arrested. He was in jail four months. He has been deserted by his family. When the disturbance occurred he was Marshal of his town. Today he lives in Nazareth, poor, deserted, faithful. But what cares he for this suffering, poverty and desertion as he contemplates the fact that he has set a torch of eternal light in his community. The church which he finally established will bear faithful witness in spite of hardships long after all persecution has ceased, and he, himself, has gone home to God.

It was our good fortune to visit the little town of Cabo (which means Cape), two hours' ride from Pernambuco, where we have a small church, organized about two years ago. We were entertained in the home of a mechanic who superintends the bridge construction along the railroad which passes through the town. He takes his Bible with him when he goes to work, and wherever he is he preaches the gospel. He told us of two station agents along the line who had recently accepted Christ through his personal efforts.

We had a delightful service that night in the church, a great throng of people being present, six of whom made public profession of their faith in Jesus. After we had returned from the church we sat in the little dining room in the rear part of this man's house until a late hour. Some of those who had suffered for the cause of the gospel came in to see us, and as we sat there in the dim light of the flickering candle, they told us of some of their sufferings for the gospel's sake. The scene reminded me of what must have taken place often in many a dark room in the early centuries when the Christians gathered together for the sake of comforting each other in their trials.

Amongst those who were present in this little room was brother Honofre, through whose efforts the church at Cabo had been founded. Several years ago he began to read a Bible which had been presented to him by a man who was not interested in it. He became converted along with his household. There was a Catholic family living opposite to him which he determined to reach with the gospel. After awhile this family accepted Christ and the two families began to hold worship in their homes. Soon they rented a hall, with the aid of a few others, and sent to Pernambuco for a missionary to come and organize them into a church. This man has endured cruel hardships. He had to abandon his business as a street merchant because the people boycotted him. He rented a house, built an oven and began to bake bread. Not long after that he was put out of this house. Again and yet again he had the same experience until recently he has rented a house from the same man who provided for our church building. He can now make a living.

The church has had experience similar to that of its founder. It was put out of three rented buildings at the instance of the Vicar, who either forced the owners to eject or he, himself, bought the property. Finally a man who is not a believer, but whose mother is, bought the present building and sold it to me church. He is permitting the church to pay for the building in installments of small sums. At last the church has a place upon which it can rest the sole of its feet and in two years has grown from ten to fifty members. On the occasion of our visit six more made public confession of Christ before a large audience and were received for baptism.

Out on the cape is a fine lighthouse which we had admired as we came up the coast on the ship. May it be a symbol of the lighthouse which this church may become to the storm tossed in that section of Brazil.

Of course, persecution is a painful thing for those who are called upon to endure it, but wherever I found those who had passed through afflictions they counted it all joy to suffer for the cause of Christ, and whenever I attempted to comfort them because of their hardships, I came away more comforted than they, for the reason that their joyous willingness to suffer for His sake strengthened my own faith and assured me of the ultimate triumph of the gospel through the labors of such heroic people. Persecution, while it may temporarily suspend work in a certain place, always defeats its own purpose, and instead of preventing the spread of the gospel, is one of the most helpful agencies in the growth of the truth.

A most encouraging illustration of this fact occurred in Pernambuco in 1904. There had been a bitter persecution at Cortez, a village not far from Pernambuco. The chief instigator of the trouble was the parish priest. The believers were driven out of the town and their lives threatened. The missionary went and was also driven out, but returned under the protection of some soldiers and conducted gospel services through a whole week in order to give courage to the believers and to demonstrate that the Protestants could not be driven out. A news account of this persecution was published in a daily paper in Pernambuco. A boy cut this article out and gave it to his teacher, a priest in the Silesian College. The teacher read the article and wrote a letter to Missionary Cannada and asked him to come to the college at midnight to explain the gospel. Two letters were passed before the missionary finally went at midnight to hold a conference. The priest came out and discussed the gospel with the missionary and then returned to the college, taking with him a copy of the New Testament. After a month the missionary went again at midnight to the college and the priest came away with him once for all. The priest went to the home of the missionary and for two months studied the Bible, after which time he was converted. He at once began to preach the gospel to his friends as he would meet them on the streets. He also made a public declaration of his conversion in print. The President of the college from which he had gone obtained an interview with him and offered him every inducement to return. His parents disinherited him and many other trials came to him, but through all, he stood firm. He has just graduated from the Southern Baptist Theological Seminary, taking the Th. D. degree and has been appointed to teach in the Baptist College and Theological Seminary in

Rev. T. B. Ray

Rio. His name is Piani. About a year after Piani's conversion he induced another priest to leave the same college. This man spent a month in the missionary's house studying the Bible, but was enticed back by the priests and hurried away to New York in order that he might escape the influence of Piani. Three months after reaching New York he was converted and joined the Fifth Avenue Baptist Church and is today a pastor of a Baptist church in Massachusetts.

In no place where our people have endured persecution, even though it may have been severe enough to cost the lives of some, has the work been abandoned, but in every place the weak, struggling congregation which faced obliteration at the fury of its enemy, has in the end increased, and today enjoys the blessing of growth in numbers and in the sympathy of the people. Persecution is a good agency in the spread of the gospel.

CHAPTER XIII

THE BIBLE AS A MISSIONARY FACTOR

The Bible is a mighty factor in the spread of the gospel in Brazil. In 1889 there came down to Bahia a man named Queiroz from two hundred and fifty miles in the interior. He came seeking baptism at the hands of Dr. Z. C. Taylor. It appears that some six or eight years previous to that time an agent of a Bible society had entered this man's community, preached the gospel and left behind him some copies of the Scriptures. One of these Bibles was found afterwards by Queiroz, who studied it and was impressed with its truth. He began to bring the message of the Word to the attention of his large circle of friends and kindred. Having preached in several places, he was finally asked by the district judge to come to his house where he was given opportunity to meet a number of friends. The friends of Queiroz, however, began to ask him whether it was right for him to be preaching thus before he had been baptized, whereupon he resolved to go to Bahia to seek baptism. He made the journey and was baptized. A week after he had returned he wrote to Dr. Taylor, saying he had preached at Deer Forks and had baptized eight. During the next two weeks similar letters were sent, which gave the number he had baptized. The church at Bahia was apprized of conditions, and it decided to send Queiroz an invitation to come and receive ordination.

Rev. T. B. Ray

He came with great humility and joy and was ordained, but before the ordination had taken place he had already baptized fifty-five people. The church, at Bahia, after the ordination of Queiroz, legalized the baptisms.

Five years after the baptism of this man Dr. Taylor was finally able to make the journey to Conquista, where he found the church well organized, with a house of worship built at its own expense and with the pastor's home erected near by. The missionary says, "I now understand why God never permitted me to visit Conquista during these five years. I believe it was for the purpose of showing me that the native Christians can and will take care of themselves and the gospel if we will only confide in them. I wonder how many churches in the United States have built their own house and pastorium and sustained themselves from the start? Not a cent from the Board has been spent on the church and the evangelization done by Brother Queiroz."

Another example of the power of the Bible in spreading the gospel is found in the way the gospel came to Guandu, State of Rio, and the country round about. One night in Campos in 1894, after the missionary had finished his sermon, a young woman approached him and said, "My father has been teaching us out of that same book you used. Would you not like to go out in the country to visit him?" The missionary replied that he would, and then the girl explained how the Bible came to this community.

One evening a colporteur approached her father's door and asked for entertainment, saying he had been refused by several families along the way. To the host's inquiry as to why he had been refused entertainment for the night the colporteur said: "They declined because I am a Protestant." The man replied. "Come in and welcome." After the dinner Mr. Vidal (for that was the farmer's name) asked what this

Protestantism meant. The colporteur explained and preached the gospel to the best of his ability.

When the time came to retire the colporteur said, "It is my custom to read the Scriptures and to pray before I retire. If you have no objection I would like to do so tonight." Mr. Vidal answered, "I shall be glad for you to do so." The colporteur read and there in the dining hall before the curious onlookers knelt and poured out his heart to his Heavenly Father. He called down the blessing and the favor of God upon the family. The tears poured down his cheeks as he lifted his soul in this prayer. After he finished praying Mr. Vidal said, "I have never heard prayer like that. Teach me how to do it. I have heard Latin prayers repeated, but they did not grip me like that." The colporteur replied by explaining that prayer must be from the heart. He then took out a Bible and said, "I want to make you a present of this book. You have been kind to me. Read it, for it has in it the Word of Life." He went away the following morning. We do not know who he was—only the record on high will discover his person to us.

The book left behind became a great light for Mr. Vidal. He read it and was so impressed with its teachings that he taught the Word to his family and neighbors. His house became a house of prayer and teaching. When Missionary Ginsburg went out there, preached the Word and explained about Christ, he asked those who wished to follow the Lord to stand. Practically the whole company stood. They had been prepared, by Mr. Vidal The missionary went back a few times and soon a church of about forty members was organized and was called the Church of Guandu.

The Word spread up the country first amongst Mr. Vidal's relatives and friends. At Santa Barbara the station master, Carlos Mendonca, was converted, who is now pastor of our church at Cantagallo. He first moved to Rio Bonito and founded a church there, the truth spread, in other directions also and so the light which the unknown colporteur left with this farmer has shed its rays of blessings upon a whole county. Twenty-one years ago, a Bible which belonged to a Catholic priest, or rather a part of a Catholic Bible, fell into the hands of the old man, Joaquim Borges. Through the reading of this Bible, he abandoned idolatry and other practices of Rome and put his trust solely in the Lord Jesus for his salvation. For sixteen years he resisted all attempts of priests and others to turn him back to Rome, always giving a clear and firm testimony to the truth of the gospel. During all this time he never met with another believer. Hearing of him, E. A. Jackson wrote him to meet him in Pilao Arcado. He came 120 miles and waited twelve days for the arrival of the missionary. As Jackson had through passage to Santa Rita, he asked the captain to hold the steamer while he baptized Mr. Borges. Before administering baptism Jackson preached to the great crowd on the river bank and on the decks of the steamer. It was a solemn and beautiful sight to behold this man, seventy-seven years of age, following his Lord in baptism at his first meeting with a minister of the gospel and before a multitude which had never witnessed such a scene. Dripping from the river, Jackson welcomed him into the ranks of God's children. The missionary embarked on the steamer and Mr. Borges went back to work among his neighbors. Up till the present time not even a native minister has visited him, for the lack of workers and funds to send them. Eye hath not seen, nor ear heard, nor hath it entered into the heart to conceive the glorious things God has prepared for the man who will go to work for Him among the neglected people of the interior of Brazil.

In the State of Sao Paulo is a boy, Ramiro by name, now about thirteen years of age, the only son of parents who do not know a letter of the alphabet. Indeed, he is the only one in a large connection that has been taught to read.

The family lives about twenty miles from their market town, Mogy das Cruzes, to which they go to sell the meager fruits of their labors on the little farm. In this town they have some acquaintances, among whom is a believer whose faith had come through reading the Bible. This believer one day came into possession of a Bible which he didn't need, and so he gave it to Ramiro, who was then about nine or ten years of age and was beginning to learn to read. The little fellow trudged home, twenty miles away, carrying his priceless present, and showed it joyously to his parents. This was the first book that ever entered their humble home, excepting, of course, Ramiro's little school book. Curious to know what the book contained, the father put Ramiro to deciphering some of its pages. Guided, no doubt, by the Holy Spirit, he fell upon the New Testament and laboriously read on and on for months and months The neighbors—all ignorant alike—would come and listen to Ramiro spell out sentence after sentence, he becoming more expert as the days went by. He would read, they would listen and discuss, the Holy Spirit, in the meantime, fixing the sacred truth in their hearts. This persistent reading of the Word went on for two or three years to a time when the Lord opened to Dr. J. J. Taylor, of Sao Paulo, a door of opportunity in Mogy das Cruzes. He found twelve people ready to follow on in the Lord's ordinance.

Since that time even more abundant fruit has been gathered. Dr. Taylor at first baptized three of Ramiro's cousins who hail from the same village twenty miles away and recently he baptized the uncle, aunt, some more cousins and Ramiro himself. Ramiro taught the words of many hymns to his family and neighbors. Through him and his book his aged grandparents, ninety years old and bedridden, rejoice in the Savior.

How great must be the might of the Word of God which can convert to salvation strong men through the faltering lips of a child And yet, after all, is not this the combination which alone is powerful in spreading the gospel—a simple, child-like heart, through which the Word may speak forth? "A little child shall lead them," because it can be artless enough to give simple utterance to the Word of God. Oh, for more in all lands who will give unaffected voice to the Word of God! That message has power in it if it can get sincere expression.

We need to realize more than we do the transcendent importance of giving wide circulation to the Bible in foreign lands. The illustrations given here of the wonderful success of the Book should help us to reach a better appreciation of the value of the Word of God in mission endeavor. Certainly, there is marvelous power in it. Its enemies fear its might; therefore, they fight desperately to prevent the circulation of it. Would that we could have as keen a realization of the vitality of this Book as do its enemies. Surely then, we would do far more for the sowing of the Scriptures beside all waters.

CHAPTER XIV

THE METTLE OF THE NATIVE CHRISTIAN

In 1894, Francisco da Silva, soon after his conversion in Bahia, went to Victoria in the State of Espirito Santo to live. He went into the interior with some surveyors, and in addition to the work he was called upon to do, he found time to tell the story of Jesus. Eight people were converted and he wrote Dr. Z. C. Taylor to come and baptize them.

Dr. Taylor was not able to go immediately, and one of the men secured his baptism in a very unique way. He asked Francisco to baptize him Francisco replied that he could not because he was not ordained. The man returned home and examined his Bible and came back a few days later and demanded again that Francisco baptize him. Francisco replied that in order to baptize, one must be ordained. "No," said the man, "I have looked in the Bible and I do not find it necessary for one to be ordained in order to baptize." So catching hold of Francisco, he pulled him along to a river near by, Francisco through it all holding back the best he could and arguing with the man that he could not baptize him. But the man constrained him and forced him into the river. Francisco seeing his zeal, performed the ceremony. Some question afterward was raised about the validity of this baptism, and the man was baptized regularly by the same

Francisco, who had in the meantime received ordination.

When he had finished with one party of surveyors another wanted to employ him, and they went to the first party to find out about him. The men said: "He has fine qualifications for the position, but there is one objection to him—he is a Protestant." "Ah, said the second party, "can't we with a little money get that out of him?" "No," replied the first, "it seems to be grown into him." He was taken by the second party, the chief of which and all his family soon became devoted Christians.

The desire to tell the story of Jesus burned in Francisco's heart so warmly that he gave up his lucrative employment with the surveying party, bought a mule and other necessities for his journey and started out to proclaim the unsearchable riches of Christ to the people of that State. He was remarkably successful and soon gathered about him a little band of believers, who, because of their faithfulness to Christ, were called upon to suffer severe persecution. They were compelled to flee into the distant mountains where Missionary Jackson afterward found them, organized them into a church and baptized seventy-five converts. Later they were able to return to their homes, due to the fact that a more lenient administration was inaugurated in Victoria. Very soon afterward our faithful missionary, L. M. Reno, was sent to this State, and the work from this good beginning has had remarkable prosperity. The pioneer missionary, da Silva, after having gained the title of Apostle to the State of Espirito Santo, was called in 1910 to his reward.

From what we have been saying, you have no doubt made many inferences about the kind of Christians these Brazilians make. If you had seen them face to face, you would have been, as I was, impressed with their appearance. They were the best-looking people I saw. Their countenances were clearer and there was a hopeful, resourceful look upon them that was not noticeable upon the non- believers. Sin and fear always break the spirit of men, and though there may be a brave look assumed, yet there always hangs a cloud over the countenance of the sin-stained and fear-driven man, be he a religionist or atheist. This change in appearance is produced by a change in their way of living. When they are converted they cease drinking, gambling, Sabbath-breaking, and often the men give up smoking and the women cease taking snuff. The fact is they sometimes are extreme upon this subject. I heard of one church that made the giving up of tobacco and another the laying aside of jewelry the test of fellowship. These people coming out from under the domination of a religion of fear into the light and liberty of the gospel are changed from glory to glory, having upon them the light of God's countenance.

They are liberal givers. There is a much larger proportion of tithers among them than among the Christians in the States. Here, too, they often go to extremes. More than one church in Brazil makes tithing obligatory upon its members. Last year the Brazilian Baptists gave as much per capita for foreign missions as did the Baptists in our Southern States. They have set their aim this year higher than the Southern Baptists have. They sustain foreign mission work in Chili and Portugal. They engage in this foreign mission endeavor because the leaders think that the foreign mission principle is vital to the life and development of the churches. This giving to foreign missions is not to the neglect of their home enterprises. They have Home and State Mission Boards which they support liberally. They have am Education Board to which they gave forty cents per capita last year and all of this giving out of such grinding poverty!

Here and there are people of larger means who are munificent in their gifts. It was the generous offer of $5,000 by Captain Egydio that made possible the founding of the Collegio Americano Egydio, which school was established by the Taylors in Bahia. He paid $650 the first installment upon the furniture, but his sudden taking off prevented the college from realizing the whole amount promised, because the family lost so heavily by persecution after the father had been taken away. Col Benj. Nogueira Paranagua, a rich cattleman, built a church, school and library building at Corrente in the State of Piauhy at his own expense and afterward paid the salary of a teacher for the school. When the church in San Fidelis, which was established in the face of trying persecution, was considering how it could possibly build a meeting house, a coffee farmer, who was not yet a member, rose and said: "I am old and useless, but I want to do something for Jesus and His church. I, therefore, offer to erect the church building and the church may pay me six per cent. annually until I die, and then the building will belong to the church as a legacy which I intend to leave." As the work on the house progressed he signified his desire to be the first one to be baptized in the baptistry. This was granted gladly and his thought of charging six per cent on the building until his death disappeared in the watery grave and he made the church a present outright of the beautiful chapel. Not only this chapel has been built by an individual, but others have been built in the same way. Usually, however, the churches are built out of the sacrificial offerings of the people. So well has this church building movement progressed that now about one-third of the 142 Baptist Churches organized in Brazil worship in their own buildings, and with a few exceptions, these buildings have been erected by the gifts of the people and not by the gifts of the Foreign Mission Board. The Presbyterians show a better proportion of buildings than this and the Methodists quite as good.

The subject of self-support is a live one. There has been good progress made in this matter, but, of course, it will require many years to teach the churches their full duty in this regard. Many churches have reached the point where they take care of all local expenses. Some of the missionaries go so far as to advocate not organizing any more churches until the congregations can be self- supporting. The South Brazilian Mission, in its recent meeting, adopted the rule that no church should be organized hereafter until it could pay at last 60 per cent of its own expenses—these expenses to include the care of the house, the salary of the native pastor, etc.

I have already cited instances of personal work. I wish to say more particularly that the great success which has attended the work in Brazil must be in a large measure attributed to the fact that those who have been led to Christ have been zealous in witnessing personally to others of the grace which had been bestowed upon them.

One of the greatest laymen in Brazil is our Brother Thomaz L. da Costa. He is the Superintendent of a very considerable business firm in Bahia. He is a deacon in the First Baptist Church, one of the moving spirits upon the Brazilian Foreign Mission Board and practically superintends the work of the State Mission Board of Bahia.

Years ago he was converted in Rio through the agency of his washerwoman. This faithful woman is a member of the First Baptist Churoh. She decided she would attempt to lead Thomaz to Christ. So on Saturday when she would bring his laundry she would invite him to come to her house on the following day for dinner. I might say by way of parenthesis, that there is not a steam laundry in Brazil. All of the laundry work is done by hand. Sometimes there is quite a considerable firm which employs many laundresses. Thomaz, after declining the good woman's invitation many times, finally one day decided he would accpt. it.

On Sunday he appeared at her house for dinner. After the dinner was over she suggested that they, in company with several of her children, should take a stroll through some of the parks. They passed through the great park in the center of the city, and after a while they found themselves in front of a building in which they heard singing. The good woman suggested that they go upstairs into the hall from which proceeded the sounds of the music. They went in, Thomaz not knowing what sort of place it was. Dr. Bagby, the first missionary of our board to Brazil, was conducting a service and soon began a sermon which impressed Thomaz very greatly. The sermon drew such a picture of his life that he accused the woman of having told Dr. Bagby about him. She had not done so, she declared, and this fact impressed Thomaz even more.

Next Saturday, when she brought his laundry, she invited him to take dinner with her again on Sunday, but he was too shrewd for her and declined, saying that he understood her purpose. The message which he had heard in the sermon, however, stayed with him. On the following Saturday the good woman again invited him to take dinner with her on Sunday. He declined. When the third Saturday came, before she had time to extend her usual invitation, he said: "I am coming to dinner with you tomorrow." He went according to promise, and after the meal had been finished, they did not take a round-about course, but went directly to the church, and there the man listened to the gospel again and gave himself to Christ. He has not missed a service since unless providentially hindered. I asked him if he was sorry of the step he had taken and he replied: "No, indeed. It is as Paul says, 'A salvation not to be repented of.'"

There can be but one inevitable result to such faithful witnessing as this. One of the most hopeful signs in connection with the work in Brazil is the fact that a large percentage of the members of the churches endeavor to lead others to Christ in a personal way. A large percentage of them will conduct public services wherever the opportunity can be found. In the First Baptist Church in Rio there are more than twenty men who will go out and conduct public services. They are not skilled preachers. They may have very limited education, but they can take the Book, read it, explain its message through the light of their own individual experiences, and by this means of witnessing to the power of the saving grace of God in their own lives, they are able to lead many to Jesus. Is not this after all the kind of preaching our Lord has sent us into the world to do?

The severest persecution which these Brazilian Christians are called upon to endure is not that which comes to them when they are stoned, or when their property may be destroyed or when their business may be taken away from them through boycotts or when they may be turned into the streets through the bitter hatred of hard- hearted priests, but the most trying persecution is that which comes from the insinuating remark, the sneer of the supercilious and the doubt of the envious. The taunt of hypocrisy is often thrown into the teeth of native Christians. Their motives are frequently impugned. I was profoundly impressed with the answer they usually give to such persecutions. They reply by saying: "See how we live. Note the difference between our careers now and our careers before we became Christians." And this challenge of the life is the one which will finally answer the ridicule and doubt of all who assail them.

CHAPTER XV

THE TESTING OF THE MISSIONARY

In thinking of the missionary, most of us dwell upon the heroic self-denial he practices and the bravery with which he faces the gravest dangers. Certainly, the missionary in Brazil is due a good share of such appreciation. He has been called upon to endure shameful indignities, painful personal dangers and the enervating perils of a hostile climate. Our own missionaries have been beaten, stoned, thrown into streams, arrested and haled before courts, shot at and in many instances saved only by the most signal dispensations of Providence. Dr. Bagby, our first missionary, in spite of stoning and arrest when he was baptizing converts in Bahia, kept fearlessly on in his endeavor to lead the people to Christ. Dr. Z. C. Taylor traveled through the interior of Bahia State in perils of robbers, in perils of fanatics, in perils of infuriated priests and in perils of bloodthirsty persecutors without fear or shrinking. In the spring of 1910 Solomon Ginsburg was set upon by a mob at Itabopoana, which opened fire with such perilous directness that one bullet flattened upon the wall a few inches above his head.

This same missionary in 1894 endured bitter persecutions when he attempted to open the work at San Fidelis in the interior of the State of Rio de Janeiro. A mob of a thousand people threw stones, grass, corn and a great miscellany of other objects at him and his little band of worshipers. The howling of the mob prevented him from preaching. The best that could be done was to sing songs. Finally, a stone having struck a girl in the congregation, he carried her out through the infuriated mob to a drug store across the street, where she was resuscitated, and he returned to his service of song.

Next morning he was called to the police headquarters and the officer forbade him to preach. He asked what the missionary was doing there, to which he replied, "To preach the gospel." The missionary was then prohibited from preaching in the province. He replied that he was sorry he could not obey, for he had superior orders. He could not accept orders from the police, nor the Governor, nor even from the President of the Republic. The officer asked who this superior authority was. The missionary replied it was God. God had told him to go preach the gospel in all the world to every creature; some of God's creatures were in San Fidelis and he was there to preach according to the command of his Lord. The police officer, after plying him with insulting epithets, kept him a prisoner of the State as a disturber of the peace. On the following day he was sent to the State prison at Nictheroy, where he was confined for ten days. Friends, through the solicitation of Mrs. Ginsburg, brought pressure to bear upon the Government and the missionary was released. He was requested then as a personal favor not to return until after the naval revolt, which was then in progress, should be suppressed and a degree of quiet could be restored to the State. Being thus requested, he remained away from San Fidelis awhile.

When the revolt was suppressed he returned to San Fidelis and persecution arose again. He appealed to the chief officer of the State and fifty soldiers were sent to his relief. In choosing these fifty soldiers the officer asked for believers to volunteer. Twenty-five responded. He asked then for sympathizers and twenty- five more volunteered. These were put under the command of the missionary, who instructed them not to appear armed at the church. They came unarmed, but when the mob began to thrown stones again and refused to respect the soldiers, they pounced upon the evil doers and there was a rough and tumble fight. Several were bruised considerably and a number of limbs were broken, but after this conflict the persecution ceased.

We relate these incidents for the purpose of making it clear that our missionaries have been called upon to suffer greatly for the cause of Christ. Every missionary who has been in Brazil any length of time has felt the weight of personal, physical persecution, and all in the gravest dangers have conducted themselves as became the heroic character with which they are so splendidly endowed. And this suffering, we are sorry to say, is not yet over. For many years to come the desperate and despotic hand of Rome, which could in the name of religion invent the horrible inquisition and organize the bloodthirsty order of Jesuits, has not changed its attitude completely and will resist desperately to the last the inevitable progress of Protestantism in Brazil.

Let me hasten, however, to say that it is very easy to get the wrong impression of what the heroism of the missionary consists. It is easy for us to think it consists in his willingness to face personal danger. If such an idea should obtain amongst us permanently and alas, it has persisted altogether too long; it will rob the story of missions of its true interest and hazard appreciation of the enterprise upon the ability of the historian to find thrilling tales of adventure to gratify the appetite of the sensation-loving public.

The most trying thing to the missionary is not the imminence of personal danger, but the ever-present chilling, benumbing indifference of the people to the gospel. Even though here and there we find large numbers of people who are ready to accept the gospel, let us not deceive ourselves into the belief that all Brazil is eagerly seeking to enter the Kingdom of God. The Macedonian call to Paul did not come from a whole nation which was ready to accept his teaching, but from one man in a nation. Most all Macedonian calls are like that. The few, comparatively speaking, rise to utter such calls and these few are the keys of opportunity which may be used to unlock whole Empires. The great body of the people in Brazil (and this is especially true of the educated classes) are as indifferent to the gospel as people are most anywhere else. It is the weight of this stolid indifference which tries the endurance of the missionary. It fills the very atmosphere he breathes and hangs a dark cloud over his horizon, which only his faith in God and the winning of occasional converts graciously tinge with a silver lining. It is indifference, slowly yielding indifference that tests the temper of the missionary character. There are times when a bit of physical persecution would afford a positive relief to the fatigue of his exacting career.

The days of the pioneer missionary, with their personal dangers, have in a measure passed. The years of the persecutor in the face of an increasingly more enlightened civilization are numbered. The probability of personal perils is growing steadily less. The missionary must now fight for a hearing before a public which is too often willing to let him alone. In many places it does not care enough for his message to persecute him for bringing it. It is ready to patronize him with an assumed air of liberality and resist the message which burns in his heart and upon his lips. They are willing for him to speak, but not willing to listen to what he has to say. He must fight for a hearing with this patronizing indifference. It is this that tries his spirit. It is this that bleeds his heart of its strength. It is this that calls out the heroic in

Rev. T. B. Ray

him as never does the dart of the savage, the weapon of the fanatic or the fury of the mob. To hold on true to his purpose in the face of such soul-harrowing indifference is the crowning act of heroism upon the part of our missionaries. No one of them has ever drawn back and given up his work for fear of death at the hands of his persecutors, but it must be said for the sake of the truth that some have succumbed before the rigors of blasting indifference. The saints at home ought to support valiantly with their prayers our missionaries who at the front are engaged in a battle even unto death with indifferent souls unwilling to accept their message.

There is another count in this subject of indifference to which we at home should give more prayerful consideration. It is the failure of the churches at home to send out an adequate number of missionaries to reinforce the workers at the front and make it possible for them to take advantage of the opportunities that have come to them already. What could take the spirit out of a man more quickly than the feeling that those who had sent him out do not care enough about him to give him support and reinforcements for his work? It is a shame upon us that we at home add another burden to our missionaries by failing to loyally support them. What must be a man's thoughts after he has toiled and sacrificed on a field for years and has unceasingly begged for a mere tithe of the helpers he really needs and which we fail to send?

When that brave garrison of English soldiers were shut up in Lady Smith, South Africa, during the Boer War their courage to hold out against overwhelming odds and on insufficient rations through many weeks was kept up by the assurance that the patriotic English nation was doing its utmost to send relief, though the relief was long delayed. If the thought that their home people were not trying to send succor to them had ever taken possession of their minds, they would have surrendered forthwith. Their line of communication was cut, but they knew help was coming, and so they held out with grim determination until relief came.

How is it with our missionaries in Brazil? Their lines of communication are intact. They know their people at home are able to supply them with the help they need and yet the help does not come. What must be the conclusion forced upon, them and what must be the effect upon them? Either the churches, though able, will not give the means to send out missionaries, or the men for reinforcement will not volunteer. It may be that both causes are at work. What is the matter when a pulpit committee of a prominent church can have sixty names suggested to it of men who might become its pastor, and a good percentage (save the mark) of these direct applications, when our small missionary force in Brazil is pleading for only ten men to be sent out to relieve them in their strain? Whatever explanation we may have to offer for these things, the fact remains that our indifference to the call of our men at the front adds an additional weight to their already too heavy load, and yet, in spite of it all, they are standing with unflinching heroism at their posts.

Something must be done to relieve this situation. Counting all denominations, there are in Brazil fewer missionaries today in proportion to the population than there are either in India or China. Why this disparity of workers in Brazil? Is it because the work is not successful there? The facts show that, taking into consideration the number of workers, it is one of the most fruitful of all mission fields. Is it because there is less need of the gospel? I believe I have shown that these people are bereft of the gospel, and because of their sin and idolatry are as needy as are to be found anywhere. No, there is no excuse to be offered. Our workers at the front need help. We are trying their brave spirits by withholding the relief they have a right to expect, and yet we repeat they

Rev. T. B. Ray

are holding on with a courage that stamps them as heroes of the finest type. God help us to see our obligation to send out recruits in sufficiently large numbers to relieve these brave soldiers and transform them from a besieged garrison into an aggressive army of conquerors.

Let us bear in mind that what is said about indifference both on the foreign field and among the churches at home is spoken of the people in the large. Thank God, the light is breaking in many places at home and abroad. Many individuals and churches are today seeing the larger vision and are assuming their larger responsibility in the support of the foreign mission cause. Many are saying: "We will faithfully strengthen the hands of our brothers who toil so courageously at the front." In Brazil (and in other mission fields, too,) there is in many places a marvelous breaking away from the old attitude of indifference. The little handful of missionaries we have on the field are straining every nerve to meet the opportunities that are pressing upon them. They are not discouraged. They are as busy as life trying to meet the increasing demands. They are looking to the future with the largest hope. They are a band of the most incurable optimists you ever saw.

CHAPTER XVI

THE URGENT CALL

This very breaking away in some places is piling up additional burdens and the pitifully inadequate force is called upon to meet demands that twice their number could hardly satisfy. If we had the same distribution of Baptist ministers in our Southern country that we have in Brazil there would be only four ministers in Texas, two in Virginia, three in Georgia and other States in like proportion. Think of E. A. Nelson, the only representative of our board in the Amazon region, trying to spread himself over four States which comprise a territory five times as large as Texas. Passing down the coast, five days journey, we would find D. L. Hamilton and H. H. Muirhead, who have faced dangers as fearlessly as have any brave spirits who have enriched the annals of missionary history with courageous service. They, along with Miss Voorheis, are our sole representatives in the State of Pernambuco and in the adjoining State of Alagoas. C. F. Stapp, Solomon Ginsburg and E. A. Jackson are attempting to carry forward the work in the vast States of Piauhy, Goyaz, a part of Minas Geraes, and Bahia, which last named State has in it one city as large as New Orleans. E. A. Jackson is located far in the interior of the State, three weeks' journey from Bahia; all of the energies of Stapp are consumed in caring for the school; Ginsburg is forced to give his attention to the nurturing of the thirty-five churches and of evangelizing as far as his strength will go. In the State beyond them, going down the coast, stands L. M. Reno, in the State of Espirito Santo. In the populous State of Rio, in which is located the capital city with its 1,000,000 inhabitants, we have Entzminger, Shepard, Langston, Maddox, Cannada, Christie, Taylor and Crosland. Entzminger, in addition to conducting the publishing house, must also conduct the mission operations in Nictheroy, a city of 40,000; Shepard, Taylor and Langston have placed upon their shoulders the tremendous responsibility of conducting the college and seminary; Cannada must give his energies to the Flumenense School for Boys, leaving only Maddox, Christie and Crosland at liberty to do the wider evangelistic work and care for the many churches which the success of their labors have thrust upon them. Crosland has been transferred recently to Bello Horizonte, in the great State of Minas Geraes. Farther South, in Sao Paulo, the richest and most progressive State in the country, are Bagby, Deter and Edwards, Misses Carroll, Thomas and Grove. Bagby and wife and the young ladies just mentioned devote their time to the school, leaving only two to man a field which, because of its splendid railroad facilities, has in it scores of inviting locations for successful work. In Paranagua in the next State to the South, have been located recently R. E. Pettigrew and wife. Far down to the South in Rio Grande do Sul, a State as large as Tennessee and Kentucky combined, stands a single sentinel in the person of A. L. Dunstan. What a battle line for twenty men to maintain! It is more than 4,000 miles in length. If you should place these men in line across our Southern territory, locating the first one in Baltimore, you would travel 100 miles before you reach the second, 100 miles before you reach the third, 100 miles to the fourth, and in going toward the Southwest, you would reach the twentieth man in El Paso, Tex. Whereas, if you were to draw up the Baptist ministers enrolled in the Southern Baptist

Convention territory along the same line and pass down it to make the count, by the time you had reached El Paso you would have passed 8,000 men, for they would have been placed just one-fourth of a mile apart.

Why do we need 400 ministers in this country to one in Brazil? Is it possible that we will grudgingly cling to our 8,000 ministers and decline to give even eight to reinforce our little handful in Brazil? Such a division of forces can neither be fair nor faithful.

In drawing this picture I have practically stated the situation for the other denominations. The Presbyterians occupy the same general territory as do the Baptists with an equal number of missionaries. The Methodists have somewhat more compactly stationed about the same number of missionaries as each of the other two, while the Episcopalians, the Congregationalists and the Evangelical Mission of South America combined add a number about equal to each of the three larger denominations. A total of less than 100 ordained missionaries scattered over a territory larger than the United States of North America, which allows about four missionaries to each Brazilian State. Add to this number the wives of the missionaries, the thirty-seven unmarried women and the 125 native workers and the entire missionary body, foreign and native, barely totals 300. How utterly inadequate is such a force in the presence of such vast needs! Because this situation has in it a call so apparent and so inexpressibly urgent it is impossible to portray it in words.

The ripeness of the State of Piauhy for evangelization will illustrate the urgency of the opportunity all over Brazil. As far back as 1893 Dr. Nogueira Paranagua, who was at that time National Senator from his State, urged Dr. Z. C. Taylor to send a man into Piauhy and promised to help pay the expenses. Two years later Col. Benj. Nogueira, the brother of the Senator, gave a similar invitation, making a promise that he would sustain a missionary. It was not until 1901 that E. A. Jackson was able to reach Col. Benjamin's home. He preached the gospel in this good man's house and also in Corrente, the town near by. Persecution, bitter and determined, arose. There were three attempts to take Jackson's life in one day. Once Col. Benjamin stepped in between the assassin and the missionary and thus saved the missionary's life. Some months later, upon the return of the missionary, Col. Benjamin, who had been for so many years a friend to the gospel, gave himself to it and was baptized. In January, 1904, the new house of worship at Corrente was dedicated. It was built by Col. Benjamin at his own expense. He also built a school building and library, and afterward when the missionary was able to secure a teacher, this generous man paid all the charges.

When we reached Brazil last summer I received a message from Judge Julio Nogueira Paranagua, a nephew of Col. Benjamin, who is one of the Circuit Judges in the State of Piauhy and who after a short while is to be retired upon his pension, according to the Brazilian law. As soon as this takes place he expects to give himself entirely to the work of evangelizing his own people. The message ran: "The State of Piauhy is open to the gospel. There is a fight on between the priests and the better classes. The better educated people, disgusted with Romanism and priesthood, are drifting into materialism and atheism, but if a competent man could be situated at Therezina, the capital, the whole State could easily be won to the gospel."

His uncle, who is President of our Brazilian Convention, as we have already stated, whose family embraces in its immediate connection over a thousand people, in a letter written me after I left Rio, reinforces this appeal. He says:

"I come to call your attention to the State of Piauhy, the field in Brazil at present which seems to me to be the best prepared for evangelization. Many things have contributed to bring this about. The Masons, on the one hand, have done the most they possibly could against Romanism; on the other hand, the propaganda sincere and fervent of a small church founded in the southern part of the State, which happily is receiving the greatest blessing from Almighty God, is greatly contributing to the reception of the gospel throughout the State. My brother, Col. Benj. Nogueira, the founder of that church, has passed away, but he has left sons who are spiritual and who continue to work. With the work developed there it will spread beneficently. In the adjoining townships there exist many believers, and a church will be founded soon in Paranagua, a town situated on the beautiful lake by the same name. In the cities of Jerumenha and Floriano there are already small churches, which united to the others in assiduous labors, will powerfully contribute to the evangelization of the State, which is one of the most promising of Northern Brazil. My friend, Senator Gervazio de Britto Passo, strongly desires that a minister of the gospel come to the section where he is most influential. This Senator greatly sympathizes with our cause and is convinced that his numerous and influential friends as soon as enlightened by a pastor as to what the religion of the Baptists is, will unite with them, becoming evangelical. The best moment to move in that State is the present one, when so many causes concur for our evangelical development. The population of Piauhy, which is over 500,000, will increase considerably as well as its economic wealth.

"I hope that you will not leave this field without pastors, where the gospel is being received as the greatest benefit to which the people can aspire for their civilization."

It was my good fortune to meet the present Senator from the

State of Piauhy aboard the ship as he went up the coast, and he, while not a Protestant, urged upon me the importance of our heeding the call of this Nogueira family and personally assured me that he would do his utmost to see that such a missionary would have the widest opportunity to preach the gospel to the people. This must be a Macedonian call, which we hope to soon be able to heed.

CHAPTER XVII

THE LAST STAND OP THE LATIN RACE

There was a time in the life of the Anglo-Saxon race When it became necessary for at least a portion of it to go out into a new country in order that it might achieve the larger destiny it was to fulfill in the world. God was behind that exodus as truly as he was behind the transplanting of Abraham into a new environment. Here in our country, unfettered by despotic traditions and precedents, the Anglo-Saxon achieved religious and political liberty with a rapidity and thoroughness that could not have been possible in the old Continent of Europe.

Likewise also did God separate the Latin race from continental oppression that it might grow a better manhood in the freer atmosphere of the Western World. It is true that the Latin movement was not prompted by the same motive that impelled the Anglo-Saxon. Instead of the love of liberty, he was led out by the lure of gold. Nevertheless, we must believe the final result will be the same or else disbelieve in the ultimate triumph of the guidance of God. We should not despair of the success of this providential movement.

In South America is to be witnessed the last stand of the Latin race. There God has given him one last chance to

Rev. T. B. Ray

achieve a religious character which will honor his Lord. It is the duty of his Northern brother to sympathize with him and to believe in his ability to build up a character worthy of himself and God. If we cannot bring ourselves to such a belief it is useless for us to expect to be helpful, and it is unfaithful in us to expend money upon a people when we are confident it will be wasted.

We must not forget that these people are the descendants of the Caesars, of Seneca, Napoleon—the race that ruled the world for fifteen centuries. They surely have not lost all of their virility. It must be a case of wasted strength. We believe that this race has in it the possibility of rejuvenation. Lavaleye, the great Belgian political economist, very probably spoke the truth when he said that the Latin race is equal to the Anglo-Saxon, the only difference being the gospel which the Protestants preach and live.

We shall be helpful in our effort to give him the proper sympathy if we remember the handicaps under which he has labored. He was satisfied with his old fossilized religion, which had taught him to believe that despotism is a virtue. He did not, therefore, come to America for liberty. The early settlers were the veriest adventurers of whom the gold lust made paragons of cruelty and crime. They brought with them the intriguing priest who would corrupt the Kingdom of Heaven in order to maintain his power. There was no intentional break with their old life. The light that guided them to America was the yellow light of gold and not the white light of righteousness. The first result was that there developed in the untrammeled West the most unreasoning despotism, the most unblushing robbery and the most shamelessly corrupt priestcraft. So this whole transplanted mass of the worst intolerance, most insatiable greed and the most corrupt priesthood that Europe has ever produced, had to be taught from the beginning on the new soil, the elements of the higher manhood they so desperately needed. They had learned no first lesson in Europe, and therefore their first lesson in America was to unlearn the very things that constituted their central life and thought in Europe.

What progress has this providential teaching of the Latins in the New World made? So swiftly did they learn the lessons of liberty that hardly had the conflict which won complete freedom for the United States closed before the inevitable struggle for the same priceless heritage was in full swing in all Latin-America. And be it said to their everlasting credit that this sacred cause, in spite of revolutions and reactions, which at times hazarded the whole scheme, has made steady advance, all critics to the contrary, nothwithstanding. Political liberty is potentially at least achieved in South America. It is written in the Constitutions of the Republics and in the purposes of the people. While many battles will be fought to establish it in detail, yet the principle is so well established that it will never be uprooted, provided we give the moral and educational aid we should render at this critical hour.

We have come upon a time when we must give to our South American brothers unstinted support. They have attained political freedom, but they have not yet gained religious freedom. Nothing can be more anomolous than a State with political freedom fostering a State religion that is desperately and unscrupulously intolerant. No genuine Republic can support a State religion. The two will not live together. One or the other must go, as the history of France will abundantly substantiate. One result is inevitable—the people will eventually repudiate the despotic religion and drift into atheism and infidelity. Indeed, such a thing is happening in South America today. The better educated classes are being set hopelessly adrift religiously and the more ignorant, the common people, are following idolatry. Neither have the

Rev. T. B. Ray

gospel preached to them. The Bible is withheld. Such a state of affairs is a loud call to us.

If these people are left without a vital, character building religion they will, because of their volatile natures, degenerate into the grossest perversions of morality. In such an event the Monroe Doctrine itself would become a menace. Unless we give these people the gospel it will be far better to annul the Monroe Doctrine and permit the stronger nations of Europe to enter for the sake of good government and morality. We must either carry to our Latin brothers the regenerating, uplifting, energizing gospel of Jesus, or step out of the way and let England and Germany interpose their strong arms to prevent one of the most colossal catastrophies of all time in the moral collapse of the 70,000,000 Latin-Americans. Surely, this must be the time when we, if we ever intend to do so, must reinforce our Latin brothers. They have done well, they have made progress, but they have gone about as far as they can in the struggle upon the moral resources at their command. Their very progress in education and civilization is widening the breach between them and their former religious teachers. A new life must come in, even the power of the gospel. This alone can save Latin-America from inglorious failure.

We should not deceive ourselves into believing this prevailing religion has lost its power, even though it is losing its religious hold upon the better classes. It still retains its social influence over these same educated classes, who despise its priests. This social power is a bulwark of strength that we shall experience great difficulty in breaking. Then, too, we may be sure these Latin lands will have reinforcement from the Spanish priesthood, which fact assures a most astute clerical leadership. The Spanish priest is today the most resourceful, alert and capable priest on the earth. I believe he is to be the last strong defender of the Roman Catholic organization. It is no accident that Merry de Val, the Pope's prime minister, is a Spaniard. His appointment to that office is a just recognition of the most virile priesthood in the Roman realm. I was profoundly impressed with the Spanish priest. He looks you in the eye. He is on the street, "hail fellow well met" with the people. It is evident that he is conscious of power and possesses the gift of leadership which he is eager to use. Latin-America will feel the force of his capable leadership.

The situation in Brazil is complicated furthermore by the turn affairs have taken in Portugal. There were riots in Rio and public demonstrations against the local priests and against the exiled Portuguese priests that would probably enter Brazil after the establishment of the Portuguese Republic. But it appears that these Portuguese clerics are to be admitted. This increases the gravity of the situation. We shall be forced to take account of these men. They are a part of the religious problem of South America. Whether we wish to antagonize them or not, we shall be cognizant of their power. They will not let us alone. They will not give up South America to Protestantism without a bitter struggle.

Now I do not say all of these things of the Catholic phase of the religious problem in Latin-America for the purpose of recommending that we should gird ourselves for a polemical mission to these countries. We should look the situation squarely in the face that we may be able to estimate properly every force with which we shall have to do. I think that if the sole purpose in conducting these missions is to fight the Catholics, then we can find work to engage us more worthily. Let us evermore keep before us the fact that the Latin races have a real need of the gospel and the gospel is not being preached to them by the priests. If this is true, our duty is clear and our call is imperative. We must go and preach a positive, soul-saving gospel, avoiding conflict as far as possible and by satisfying the heart-hunger of the people with the Bread of Life, win them to Christ and a new life in Him.

I want to enter a plea for these, our brothers to the South of us. God has separated them from their old soul-dwarfing environment in Europe, and set them in this Western World that they might learn of Him. Whether they realize it or not, they are making the last fight for salvation and character their race is ever to engage in. They have a need of the gospel as distressing as that of the grossest heathen. Their religion itself is leading them further and further from their saving Lord. Their teachers, who should show them the light of life, are a beclouding hindrance. The little band of missionaries we have sent are hopelessly inadequate to the task and plead for reinforcements with a pathos that almost breaks our hearts. Oh, do not some of us, as we have followed the portrayal of the needs of South America, like Isaiah of old, hear the Lord saying, "Whom shall I send and who will go for us?" God grant that some of us may respond as he did, "Lord, here am I. Send me."

The same deep longing for salvation that is in our hearts is in the Latin heart. One day in the interior of Brazil I stood with a missionary speaking with a man who had ridden to the railroad station to talk with us a few moments while the train was stopping. As we conversed a boy twelve years of age drew near to hear us. He was pitifully disfigured with leprosy. So moved was the missionary by the sight that he turned and said: "Why do you not go somewhere and be treated." There flashed instantly in the boy's eye a hope that had long since died, and he quickly inquired, "Where can I go?" The missionary could not tell him, and I watched the last ray of hope flicker for a second and then die out forever! Ever since that day I have been hearing that pathetic question, "Where can I go?" I seem to hear all Latin-

Americans ask it out of depths of sin. And we know to whom they must go for healing and salvation. Shall we tell them? "Lord to whom shall we go—thou hast the words of eternal life." To whom shall Latin- America go? Only Christ has for them the word of life which blessed truth they will never know unless we carry it to them.

Rev. T. B. Ray

APPENDIX

SUMMARY OF SOUTHERN BAPTIST WORK IN BRAZIL

I. MISSIONARIES—

  1. Foreign, 44.

    (1) Men, 21.
    (2) Women, 23.

  2. Native, 117.

II. CHURCH STATISTICS—

  1. Churches, 142.
  2. Membership, 9,939.
  3. Church Buildings, 44.
  4. Outstations, 497.
  5. Sunday Schools, 138.
  6. Sunday School Scholars, 4,438.

III. SCHOOLS—

  1. Primary Schools, 9.
  2. Bagby School for Girls in Sao Paulo.
  3. Fluminense School for Boys in Nova Friburgo.
  4. School for Boys and Girls in Bahia.

5. School for Boys and Girls in Pernambuco.
6. Rio Baptist College and Seminary in Rio.
7. Total number of students, 869.
8. Theological Departments in connection with Rio and Penrambuco schools.

IV. GENERAL—

1. Work begun in 1882.
2. Publishing House in Rio.

Rev. T. B. Ray

Choose from Thousands of 1stWorldLibrary Classics By

A. M. Barnard
Ada Leverson
Adolphus William Ward
Aesop
Agatha Christie
Alexander Aaronsohn
Alexander Kielland
Alexandre Dumas
Alfred Gatty
Alfred Ollivant
Alice Duer Miller
Alice Turner Curtis
Alice Dunbar
Allen Chapman
Alleyne Ireland
Ambrose Bierce
Amelia E. Barr
Amory H. Bradford
Andrew Lang
Andrew McFarland Davis
Andy Adams
Angela Brazil
Anna Alice Chapin
Anna Sewell
Annie Besant
Annie Hamilton Donnell
Annie Payson Call
Annie Roe Carr
Annonaymous
Anton Chekhov
Archibald Lee Fletcher
Arnold Bennett
Arthur C. Benson
Arthur Conan Doyle
Arthur M. Winfield
Arthur Ransome
Arthur Schnitzler
Arthur Train
Atticus
B.H. Baden-Powell
B. M. Bower
B. C. Chatterjee
Baroness Emmuska Orczy
Baroness Orczy
Basil King
Bayard Taylor
Ben Macomber
Bertha Muzzy Bower
Bjornstjerne Bjornson

Booth Tarkington
Boyd Cable
Bram Stoker
C. Collodi
C. E. Orr
C. M. Ingleby
Carolyn Wells
Catherine Parr Traill
Charles A. Eastman
Charles Amory Beach
Charles Dickens
Charles Dudley Warner
Charles Farrar Browne
Charles Ives
Charles Kingsley
Charles Klein
Charles Hanson Towne
Charles Lathrop Pack
Charles Romyn Dake
Charles Whibley
Charles Willing Beale
Charlotte M. Braeme
Charlotte M. Yonge
Charlotte Perkins Stetson
Clair W. Hayes
Clarence Day Jr.
Clarence E. Mulford
Clemence Housman
Confucius
Coningsby Dawson
Cornelis DeWitt Wilcox
Cyril Burleigh
D. H. Lawrence
Daniel Defoe
David Garnett
Dinah Craik
Don Carlos Janes
Donald Keyhoe
Dorothy Kilner
Dougan Clark
Douglas Fairbanks
E. Nesbit
E. P. Roe
E. Phillips Oppenheim
E. S. Brooks
Earl Barnes
Edgar Rice Burroughs
Edith Van Dyne
Edith Wharton

Edward Everett Hale
Edward J. O'Biren
Edward S. Ellis
Edwin L. Arnold
Eleanor Atkins
Eleanor Hallowell Abbott
Eliot Gregory
Elizabeth Gaskell
Elizabeth McCracken
Elizabeth Von Arnim
Ellem Key
Emerson Hough
Emilie F. Carlen
Emily Bronte
Emily Dickinson
Enid Bagnold
Enilor Macartney Lane
Erasmus W. Jones
Ernie Howard Pie
Ethel May Dell
Ethel Turner
Ethel Watts Mumford
Eugene Sue
Eugenie Foa
Eugene Wood
Fustace Hale Ball
Evelyn Everett-green
Everard Cotes
F. H. Cheley
F. J. Cross
F. Marion Crawford
Fannie E. Newberry
Federick Austin Ogg
Ferdinand Ossendowski
Fergus Hume
Florence A. Kilpatrick
Fremont B. Deering
Francis Bacon
Francis Darwin
Frances Hodgson Burnett
Frances Parkinson Keyes
Frank Gee Patchin
Frank Harris
Frank Jewett Mather
Frank L. Packard
Frank V. Webster
Frederic Stewart Isham
Frederick Trevor Hill
Frederick Winslow Taylor

Friedrich Kerst
Friedrich Nietzsche
Fyodor Dostoyevsky
G.A. Henty
G.K. Chesterton
Gabrielle E. Jackson
Garrett P. Serviss
Gaston Leroux
George A. Warren
George Ade
Geroge Bernard Shaw
George Cary Eggleston
George Durston
George Ebers
George Eliot
George Gissing
George MacDonald
George Meredith
George Orwell
George Sylvester Viereck
George Tucker
George W. Cable
George Wharton James
Gertrude Atherton
Gordon Casserly
Grace E. King
Grace Gallatin
Grace Greenwood
Grant Allen
Guillermo A. Sherwell
Gulielma Zollinger
Gustav Flaubert
H. A. Cody
H. B. Irving
H.C. Bailey
H. G. Wells
H. H. Munro
H. Irving Hancock
H. R. Naylor
H. Rider Haggard
H. W. C. Davis
Haldeman Julius
Hall Caine
Hamilton Wright Mabie
Hans Christian Andersen
Harold Avery
Harold McGrath
Harriet Beecher Stowe
Harry Castlemon
Harry Coghill
Harry Houidini

Hayden Carruth
Helent Hunt Jackson
Helen Nicolay
Hendrik Conscience
Hendy David Thoreau
Henri Barbusse
Henrik Ibsen
Henry Adams
Henry Ford
Henry Frost
Henry James
Henry Jones Ford
Henry Seton Merriman
Henry W Longfellow
Herbert A. Giles
Herbert Carter
Herbert N. Casson
Herman Hesse
Hildegard G. Frey
Homer
Honore De Balzac
Horace B. Day
Horace Walpole
Horatio Alger Jr.
Howard Pyle
Howard R. Garis
Hugh Lofting
Hugh Walpole
Humphry Ward
Ian Maclaren
Inez Haynes Gillmore
Irving Bacheller
Isabel Cecilia Williams
Isabel Hornibrook
Israel Abrahams
Ivan Turgenev
J.G.Austin
J. Henri Fabre
J. M. Barrie
J. M. Walsh
J. Macdonald Oxley
J. R. Miller
J. S. Fletcher
J. S. Knowles
J. Storer Clouston
J. W. Duffield
Jack London
Jacob Abbott
James Allen
James Andrews
James Baldwin

James Branch Cabell
James DeMille
James Joyce
James Lane Allen
James Lane Allen
James Oliver Curwood
James Oppenheim
James Otis
James R. Driscoll
Jane Abbott
Jane Austen
Jane L. Stewart
Janet Aldridge
Jens Peter Jacobsen
Jerome K. Jerome
Jessie Graham Flower
John Buchan
John Burroughs
John Cournos
John F. Kennedy
John Gay
John Glasworthy
John Habberton
John Joy Bell
John Kendrick Bangs
John Milton
John Philip Sousa
John Taintor Foote
Jonas Lauritz Idemil Lie
Jonathan Swift
Joseph A. Altsheler
Joseph Carey
Joseph Conrad
Joseph E. Badger Jr
Joseph Hergesheimer
Joseph Jacobs
Jules Vernes
Julian Hawthrone
Julie A Lippmann
Justin Huntly McCarthy
Kakuzo Okakura
Karle Wilson Baker
Kate Chopin
Kenneth Grahame
Kenneth McGaffey
Kate Langley Bosher
Kate Langley Bosher
Katherine Cecil Thurston
Katherine Stokes
L. A. Abbot
L. T. Meade

L. Frank Baum	Paul G. Tomlinson	T. S. Arthur
Latta Griswold	Paul Severing	The Princess Der Ling
Laura Dent Crane	Percy Brebner	Thomas A. Janvier
Laura Lee Hope	Percy Keese Fitzhugh	Thomas A Kempis
Laurence Housman	Peter B. Kyne	Thomas Anderton
Lawrence Beasley	Plato	Thomas Bailey Aldrich
Leo Tolstoy	Quincy Allen	Thomas Bulfinch
Leonid Andreyev	R. Derby Holmes	Thomas De Quincey
Lewis Carroll	R. L. Stevenson	Thomas Dixon
Lewis Sperry Chafer	R. S. Ball	Thomas H. Huxley
Lilian Bell	Rabindranath Tagore	Thomas Hardy
Lloyd Osbourne	Rahul Alvares	Thomas More
Louis Hughes	Ralph Bonehill	Thornton W. Burgess
Louis Joseph Vance	Ralph Henry Barbour	U. S. Grant
Louis Tracy	Ralph Victor	Upton Sinclair
Louisa May Alcott	Ralph Waldo Emmerson	Valentine Williams
Lucy Fitch Perkins	Rene Descartes	Various Authors
Lucy Maud Montgomery	Ray Cummings	Vaughan Kester
Luther Benson	Rex Beach	Victor Appleton
Lydia Miller Middleton	Rex E. Beach	Victor G. Durham
Lyndon Orr	Richard Harding Davis	Victoria Cross
M. Corvus	Richard Jefferies	Virginia Woolf
M. H. Adams	Richard Le Gallienne	Wadsworth Camp
Margaret E. Sangster	Robert Barr	Walter Camp
Margret Howth	Robert Frost	Walter Scott
Margaret Vandercook	Robert Gordon Anderson	Washington Irving
Margaret W. Hungerford	Robert L. Drake	Wilbur Lawton
Margret Penrose	Robert Lansing	Wilkie Collins
Maria Edgeworth	Robert Lynd	Willa Cather
Maria Thompson Daviess	Robert Michael Ballantyne	Willard F. Baker
Mariano Azuela	Robert W. Chambers	William Dean Howells
Marion Polk Angellotti	Rosa Nouchette Carey	William le Queux
Mark Overton	Rudyard Kipling	W. Makepeace Thackeray
Mark Twain	Saint Augustine	William W. Walter
Mary Austin	Samuel B. Allison	William Shakespeare
Mary Catherine Crowley	Samuel Hopkins Adams	Winston Churchill
Mary Cole	Sarah Bernhardt	Yei Theodora Ozaki
Mary Hastings Bradley	Sarah C. Hallowell	Yogi Ramacharaka
Mary Roberts Rinehart	Selma Lagerlof	Young E. Allison
Mary Rowlandson	Sherwood Anderson	Zane Grey
M. Wollstonecraft Shelley	Sigmund Freud	
Maud Lindsay	Standish O'Grady	
Max Beerbohm	Stanley Weyman	
Myra Kelly	Stella Benson	
Nathaniel Hawthrone	Stella M. Francis	
Nicolo Machiavelli	Stephen Crane	
O. F. Walton	Stewart Edward White	
Oscar Wilde	Stijn Streuvels	
Owen Johnson	Swami Abhedananda	
P.G. Wodehouse	Swami Parmananda	
Paul and Mabel Thorne	T. S. Ackland